SECRETS OF THE ARCTIC

A KIDS GUIDE TO EXPLORING THE WORLD OF ICE AND POLAR BEARS

BRIAN THOMAS

1
INTRODUCTION TO THE ARCTIC

The Arctic is the region that sits at the very top of our planet. If you look at a globe, you'll see that this area is surrounded by the North Pole, and it includes parts of eight countries: Canada, the United States (Alaska), Russia, Finland, Sweden, Norway, Iceland, and Greenland. But what really makes the Arctic special isn't just where it is on the map; it's how everything here is designed to survive the extreme cold and long, dark winters. Life here has found incredible ways to make a home in the ice and snow.

Now, you might wonder why the Arctic is so cold compared to other parts of the world. It all has to do with sunlight. At the top of the Earth, sunlight hits at an angle instead of shining directly down like it does closer to the equator. This angle means the sun's warmth spreads out more, making it feel much colder. During winter, the sun even disappears for months! This period of darkness is called the polar night. Imagine a whole winter without the sun! But in the summer, the opposite happens: the sun never sets, and it shines all day and night in what's called the midnight sun. Animals, plants, and even people living here have learned to adjust to these long stretches of day and night. It's as if they're following a unique rhythm, one that the rest of the world doesn't experience.

The Arctic is filled with ice – lots and lots of it! But not all Arctic ice is the same. For example, sea ice forms on the ocean surface and can be thick or thin, depending on the time of year. Glaciers, on the other hand, are massive chunks of ice and snow that have built up over hundreds or even thousands of years. Some glaciers are so old they've seen the rise and fall of ancient civilizations. And then there are icebergs, which are pieces of glaciers that have broken off and now float in the ocean. You might have seen pictures of them before: giant, blue-white chunks of ice drifting silently in the sea. The funny thing is, most of an iceberg is hidden underwater, like a frozen mountain with only its peak sticking out.

With all this ice, you'd think the Arctic would just be one big, frozen wasteland, but there's so much more going on here. For one, the Arctic Ocean, which sits at the center of the Arctic, is home to incredible marine life. Whales, like the massive bowhead whale, swim through these cold waters, along with walruses and seals. The ice and snow may look lifeless at first, but it's actually teeming with life beneath the surface. During the brief Arctic summer, when the ice melts a bit, small plants called algae bloom under the sea ice, creating food for tiny animals called zooplankton. In turn, fish eat the zooplankton, and larger animals eat the fish. It's like a hidden feast beneath the ice!

You'll also find that life on land is surprisingly active. Sure, not many animals can survive the harsh winters, but those that do are perfectly adapted for it. Take the polar bear, for example, with its thick fur and a layer of fat that keeps it warm even in freezing temperatures. Or the Arctic fox, which changes color with the seasons – white in winter to blend in with the snow, and brown in summer to match the tundra. And there are even birds, like the snowy owl and the Arctic tern, that travel thousands of miles to come here every year.

The Arctic isn't just ice and animals, though. It's also home to people who have lived here for thousands of years. Indigenous groups like the Inuit in Canada and Greenland, and the Sámi in Norway, Sweden, Finland, and Russia, have rich cultures and traditions built around this challenging landscape. They hunt, fish, and build homes in ways that help them live comfortably, even when the temperatures drop far below freezing. Imagine having to build a house that could keep you warm through some of the coldest winters on Earth! The skills and knowledge of these communities are a big part of what makes the Arctic so unique.

And then there's the sky! The Arctic is one of the best places on Earth to see the northern lights, or aurora borealis. Imagine stepping outside on a cold, dark night, looking up, and seeing waves of green, pink, and purple light dancing across the sky. The lights are caused by particles from the sun colliding with Earth's atmosphere, creating a colorful, otherworldly glow. For many people, seeing the northern lights is a once-in-a-lifetime experience.

The Climate and Seasons

The reason for these extreme seasons has everything to do with the way Earth is tilted. Instead of standing straight up and down, our planet is tilted at a slight angle – about 23.5 degrees. Because of this tilt, different parts of the Earth get sunlight at different angles throughout the year. For most of us, this just means that our days get shorter in the winter and longer in the summer. But for the Arctic, where everything is more extreme, this tilt creates seasons where the sun either never rises or never sets.

Let's start with winter, when the Arctic enters a period known as the polar night. During the polar night, the sun dips below the horizon and doesn't come back up for weeks. For people who live in the Arctic, this time of year means constant night – it's as if someone turned off the world's light switch. In some parts of the Arctic, like the North Pole, the polar night lasts for about six months! That means half a year of complete darkness, except for a few hours of dim twilight. It's not pitch black all the time, though. When the moon is out, it can reflect off the snow and ice, making everything look almost as bright as day. And then, of course, there are the incredible northern lights, which bring color and movement to the dark Arctic skies.

But even in this long, dark winter, life goes on. Arctic animals have adapted to the polar night by sleeping more, moving around less, and relying on their other senses to find food and shelter. For example, the polar bear, one of the most famous Arctic animals, uses its powerful sense of smell to track seals under the ice. It might be dark, but that doesn't stop the polar bear from hunting. And the Arctic fox, with its keen hearing, listens for the sounds of small animals scurrying beneath the snow. While most animals would struggle to survive in the dark and freezing cold, Arctic animals seem to take it all in stride.

People in the Arctic also have their own ways of dealing with the long nights. For Indigenous groups like the Inuit, the polar night is just another part of life. They spend more time indoors, telling stories, making art, and working on traditional crafts. Imagine gathering around a cozy fire with your family, sharing stories that have been passed down for generations. For Arctic communities, these long nights are a time to come together, rest, and celebrate their culture.

And then, just when it seems like winter will never end, the sun starts to rise again. At first, it might only peek over the horizon for a few minutes each day, casting a soft glow across the landscape. Little by little, the days get longer, and the Arctic begins to wake up from its long sleep. By the time summer arrives, the Arctic is transformed. This is when something magical happens: the midnight sun.

During the Arctic summer, the sun stays in the sky all day and all night. It never sets! This phenomenon, known as the midnight sun, can last for several months, depending on how far north you go. At the North Pole, the sun stays up for a full six months, shining down on the icy landscape day after day. For people who live in the Arctic, it's like having an endless summer day. Imagine playing outside at midnight, with the sun shining as bright as noon – it's as if time itself has been stretched out, letting you do more and see more than you ever could anywhere else.

This endless daylight creates a burst of activity across the Arctic. Animals come out of hiding, plants begin to grow, and the ice starts to melt. The Arctic fox, which spent the winter huddled in its den, now roams freely, hunting and exploring under the midnight sun. Migratory birds, like the Arctic tern, fly thousands of miles to nest and raise their young in the Arctic's warm summer months. And fish, insects, and tiny plants called algae thrive in the sunlight, creating a rich ecosystem that feeds animals all the way up the food chain.

The midnight sun also has a big impact on people's lives. For Arctic communities, this is a time of celebration and activity. Fishing, hunting, and gathering become much easier in the constant daylight. Some people might even work and play late into the night, taking advantage of the sun's energy. Just as the polar night brings families together indoors, the midnight sun brings people outdoors, where they can enjoy the land and all it has to offer. Festivals, games, and ceremonies fill the summer months, as everyone makes the most of the warm, bright season.

Yet even with all this sunlight, the Arctic doesn't get hot. In fact, temperatures often stay pretty chilly, even in the middle of summer. The reason is that the sun's rays still hit the Arctic at an angle, just like they do in winter. This means that, while it's warmer than during the polar night, the Arctic summer is still cool compared to summers elsewhere. The sun might be shining, but the snow and ice don't melt completely. This balance between light and cold is what makes the Arctic so unique – it's a place of extremes, but everything works together in harmony.

Why Explore the Arctic?

Why would anyone want to explore a place as cold, dark, and extreme as the Arctic? This frozen land of ice and snow may seem empty and quiet from afar, but it's actually filled with mysteries and wonders waiting to be uncovered. The Arctic holds secrets that go back thousands of years, from the history of ancient explorers to incredible wildlife, to how our planet's climate works. For scientists, adventurers, and people who just love discovering new things, the Arctic is like a giant puzzle. Each piece reveals something new about our world.

One of the biggest reasons to explore the Arctic is because it's one of the least understood regions on Earth. Think about it: most people live far away from this icy area, and its harsh environment makes it difficult to study. But that's also why it's so exciting. The Arctic is like a hidden world, one that can teach us so much if we're willing to brave its challenges.

Even today, scientists and explorers are constantly finding new things here. They study the ice, the animals, the weather, and even the ground beneath the snow. Each discovery brings us closer to understanding how this place affects the rest of the planet.

The Arctic also plays a huge role in regulating Earth's climate. All the ice and snow here reflect sunlight, which helps keep our planet cool. When the Arctic warms up and some of this ice melts, it can have a big impact on weather patterns around the world. Scientists study this process closely, measuring the ice, the temperature, and the way Arctic sea levels rise and fall. By exploring the Arctic, they can learn more about climate change and how it affects everything, from the weather we experience every day to the future of our oceans.

Beyond climate science, the Arctic is home to incredible animals that can't be found anywhere else. Imagine seeing a polar bear up close, with its thick, creamy white fur and powerful paws made for walking on ice. Or spotting a narwhal, the "unicorn of the sea," with its long, spiraled tusk sticking out like a lance. Narwhals are mysterious creatures that spend most of their lives in deep, icy waters, making them hard to study. And then there's the Arctic fox, which changes colors with the seasons, blending into the snow in winter and the tundra in summer. Studying these animals helps scientists understand how life adapts to such extreme conditions and offers clues about how different species have evolved to survive in different parts of the world.

The Arctic is also one of the best places to study the effects of seasonal changes on plants and animals. Because the Arctic's seasons are so extreme – months of darkness followed by months of endless daylight – the plants and animals here have unique ways of surviving. During the summer, when the midnight sun shines, small plants and flowers bloom across the tundra, creating bursts of color against the white snow. Birds like the Arctic tern fly thousands of miles to take advantage of this brief period of warmth and food. And when winter returns, animals prepare in fascinating ways, either by migrating to warmer places or hunkering down to wait out the cold. By exploring the Arctic, scientists can learn more about how seasons affect life cycles, and what that means for other parts of the world as our climate changes.

And then there are the mysteries of the Arctic's human history. Indigenous groups like the Inuit and the Sámi have lived here for thousands of years, developing skills and traditions that allow them to thrive in this challenging environment. They've passed down stories, hunting techniques, and survival skills from generation to generation, and their knowledge of the land is unmatched. For centuries, Arctic explorers from other parts of the world have tried to map this region and understand its people. Some explorers, like the famous Norwegian Fridtjof Nansen, ventured deep into the Arctic on daring expeditions, risking their lives to bring back information about this unknown land. Today, archaeologists and historians continue to study the remains of these early journeys, searching for clues about how people have interacted with the Arctic over time.

Another mystery that draws people to the Arctic is its hidden geology. Beneath all that ice and snow, there's an ancient landscape of mountains, valleys, and rivers that's been carved out by glaciers over millions of years. Geologists use special tools to study the Arctic's frozen ground, called permafrost, which holds ancient plant material and fossils that can teach us about Earth's history. Imagine finding the bones of a woolly mammoth, perfectly preserved in the ice! This permafrost also holds valuable information about past climates, helping scientists understand how our world has changed over time and what it might look like in the future.

The Arctic even has secrets about outer space! Because the Arctic is so far north, it's one of the best places on Earth to see the northern lights, or aurora borealis. When particles from the sun collide with Earth's atmosphere, they create beautiful, dancing lights in shades of green, pink, and purple. The aurora borealis is like a natural light show, one that has fascinated people for centuries. Indigenous stories often speak of these lights as the spirits of ancestors or animals, moving across the sky. Studying these lights helps scientists understand more about our planet's atmosphere and how it interacts with the sun's energy. For astronomers and space scientists, the Arctic is like a giant observatory, where they can see and measure things that are hard to observe anywhere else.

Exploring the Arctic isn't easy, though. The cold, the ice, and the remote locations make it one of the most challenging places to study. Researchers often have to live in small, isolated research stations, far away from home, and they need special equipment to stay safe and warm. They use helicopters, icebreakers, and snowmobiles to get around, and they have to be prepared for blizzards, freezing temperatures, and unpredictable weather. But despite the challenges, many scientists and explorers are drawn to the Arctic for its beauty and the sense of adventure it offers. There's something about standing on the edge of a frozen sea, with nothing but ice stretching out in all directions, that captures the imagination.

2

A BRIEF HISTORY OF ARCTIC EXPLORATION

Long before ships sailed through icy waters or scientists set up research stations in the Arctic, this frozen region was already home to people who knew its secrets well. These people were the ancestors of today's Inuit and other Indigenous groups who lived in the Arctic for thousands of years. Their knowledge of the land, the animals, and how to survive in one of the coldest places on Earth is remarkable. Imagine a place where temperatures can drop below freezing for most of the year, where the ground is often covered in ice and snow, and yet these people not only survived but built rich, thriving cultures. They didn't just pass through the Arctic; they called it home.

The Inuit are one of the most well-known

Indigenous groups of the Arctic. Today, they live in regions like northern Canada, Greenland, and parts of Alaska. But their ancestors traveled far and wide, adapting to the Arctic landscape as they went. Long ago, around 5,000 years back, these early Arctic peoples started to move into this harsh environment. They learned to use the land and resources around them to survive, developing skills that they passed down through generations. These skills weren't just about staying alive; they were about understanding and respecting the Arctic.

The early Inuit didn't have big houses, warm clothing stores, or grocery markets to rely on. Instead, they built their lives around the resources they could find. They wore thick fur clothing made from animals they hunted, like seals and caribou, to keep warm in the freezing weather. Every piece of clothing had a purpose, from the boots called *kamiks*, made of sealskin, to the warm, double-layered parkas they wore. They even had special ways of making their clothes so they'd be water-resistant, which was really important in a place with so much ice and snow.

But how did they build shelters in a land where trees were scarce, and the ground was often too frozen to dig? They used what the land provided: ice and snow. Some groups, like the Inuit, built *igloos* from blocks of compacted snow, creating strong, insulated structures that kept out the cold. Snow might seem like an unusual building material, but it actually makes a good insulator. Inside an igloo, the temperature could be much warmer than it was outside, which made it a cozy refuge during the harsh winter months. Other times, they set up tents made from animal hides during the warmer months, when they moved around to follow the animals they hunted.

Hunting was a central part of life for the Inuit and other Indigenous Arctic groups. With limited plant life available, they relied heavily on animals for food, clothing, and tools. Seals, whales, walruses, and caribou were essential. Each hunt was more than just gathering food; it was a skill passed down, a lesson in survival, and a way to connect with their ancestors. Hunting also required a deep knowledge of the Arctic landscape and its wildlife. For example, seals would come up to breathe through holes in the ice, and hunters would wait patiently by these holes, sometimes for hours, until a seal surfaced.

But the Inuit didn't hunt alone. They had help from some special four-legged friends – the hardworking and loyal sled dogs. These dogs were not just pets; they were partners. They helped pull sleds over the ice and snow, carrying supplies and people across long distances. A sled dog team could make the difference between surviving the Arctic journey and getting stranded. The bond between the Inuit and their dogs was strong, built on trust and teamwork. Even today, dog sledding remains an important part of Inuit culture.

Inuit families and communities were close-knit, and everyone had a role to play. Children learned survival skills from a young age, watching and helping their parents and elders. They learned to sew clothes from animal hides, to hunt, to fish, and to build shelters. They listened to stories that taught them about the land, the animals, and the spirits that were believed to live in everything around them. These stories weren't just entertainment; they were a way to pass down knowledge, to share wisdom, and to keep their culture alive.

Stories were a huge part of life for Indigenous Arctic people. Through storytelling, they shared their beliefs about the world, the spirits, and the forces of nature. One common belief among the Inuit was that every animal, every rock, and even the wind and water had a spirit. They believed that treating these spirits with respect would keep them safe and bring them good fortune in hunting and survival. Imagine standing under the vast Arctic sky, listening to a story about the northern lights – those colorful, dancing lights that fill the Arctic night – and learning that some people believed they were the spirits of ancestors, watching over them from above.

These beliefs shaped how the Inuit treated the land and the animals they depended on. They believed in using every part of an animal they hunted, making sure nothing was wasted. If they hunted a caribou, they would use its meat for food, its bones for tools, its fur for clothing, and even its sinew (a strong, flexible tissue) for sewing. This respect for nature and understanding of their environment helped them survive in a place where resources were limited and winters were long.

The Arctic might seem like a lonely place, but the early Inuit were connected to other Indigenous groups across the region. They traded with neighboring tribes, exchanging goods like furs, tools, and even food. This trade allowed them to share knowledge and resources, building a network of relationships that stretched across the Arctic. Even though they lived in different areas and had different customs, these Indigenous groups shared a respect for the land and a deep understanding of how to live in harmony with it.

Famous Arctic Explorers

One of the earliest and most famous Arctic explorers was Erik the Red, a Norse explorer who lived over a thousand years ago. Erik wasn't just any adventurer – he was a Viking, known for his fiery temper and his daring spirit. After being banished from Iceland for a series of disputes (and even some violent fights), Erik sailed west, looking for new lands. This led him to Greenland, where he became one of the first Europeans to settle in the Arctic. He named it "Greenland" as a way to attract more settlers, even though much of it was covered in ice. Erik's journey to Greenland opened the door for future Viking exploration of the Arctic and even led his son, Leif Erikson, to reach North America long before Columbus.

Erik's journey was just the beginning. Centuries later, as the world's maps were being drawn and redrawn, European explorers became more interested in the Arctic. They wanted to find a route to Asia that would allow them to trade for valuable goods like spices and silk. This desire led to the search for the fabled Northwest Passage, a route through the Arctic Ocean that would connect the Atlantic and Pacific Oceans. Many explorers tried to find this route, and many failed – but their journeys taught the world a lot about the Arctic.

One famous explorer who ventured into the Arctic was Sir John Franklin, a British naval officer known for his determination. In 1845, he led an expedition with two ships, the HMS Erebus and HMS Terror, to finally map out the Northwest Passage. Franklin's ships were well-equipped with the best technology of the time, and his crew of 129 men were ready for the journey. But the Arctic wasn't an easy place to explore. As the ships sailed deeper into the ice, they became trapped, unable to move forward or back. Franklin and his crew faced freezing temperatures, dwindling supplies, and dangerous ice. They never returned, and their fate remained a mystery for over a century.

People searched for Franklin and his crew for years, and their story became one of the Arctic's most famous mysteries. It wasn't until recent years that researchers finally located the wrecks of the Erebus and Terror, frozen and preserved on the seafloor. Franklin's expedition taught the world just how dangerous the Arctic could be – and how much planning and bravery it would take to explore it.

While explorers like Franklin were motivated by the promise of new trade routes, others were driven by scientific curiosity. One of the most famous scientific explorers of the Arctic was Fridtjof Nansen, a Norwegian explorer who had a deep love for both science and adventure. Nansen wasn't just interested in mapping the Arctic; he wanted to understand how its ice, weather, and sea currents worked. In 1893, Nansen set out on a daring journey aboard his ship, the Fram, hoping to reach the North Pole.

Nansen's plan was both bold and risky. He deliberately allowed the Fram to become trapped in the Arctic ice, hoping that the natural movement of the ice would carry him closer to the pole. This strategy meant that Nansen and his crew would be frozen in place for months, maybe even years, as they drifted with the ice. They faced endless darkness, isolation, and the constant threat of being crushed by shifting ice. But Nansen was prepared. He designed the Fram to be incredibly sturdy, with a rounded shape that would allow it to ride up on the ice instead of being crushed. Nansen and his crew spent three years in the Arctic, conducting scientific observations and gathering valuable data. Although they didn't reach the North Pole, Nansen's expedition was a major success, proving that it was possible to survive and even study the Arctic for long periods.

As the 20th century approached, explorers around the world set their sights on reaching the North Pole itself – the "top of the world." One of the most famous attempts was led by American explorer Robert Peary. Peary had spent years exploring the Arctic and was determined to be the first person to reach the pole. In 1909, after several failed attempts, he claimed to have reached the North Pole, along with his assistant Matthew Henson and a team of Inuit guides. Peary's claim was controversial, and some people doubted whether he had actually reached the pole. Still, his journey marked an important moment in Arctic exploration, and his use of Inuit survival techniques, like traveling with dog sleds and wearing fur clothing, showed that knowledge from Indigenous peoples was essential for surviving the Arctic.

While these early explorers relied on ships, sleds, and courage, modern Arctic explorers have the advantage of advanced technology. Scientists today use icebreakers, which are powerful ships that can cut through thick ice, allowing them to travel to parts of the Arctic that were once unreachable. They use satellites to map the landscape, drones to study wildlife from above, and underwater robots to explore beneath the ice. But even with all this technology, the Arctic remains challenging and full of surprises.

One modern explorer who stands out is Pen Hadow, a British polar explorer known for his solo journey to the North Pole in 2003. Hadow walked, skied, and swam through the icy waters alone, becoming the first person to reach the pole without being resupplied along the way. His journey was grueling, filled with encounters with dangerous ice, freezing water, and unpredictable weather. Hadow's expedition showed the world just how much dedication and resilience it takes to explore the Arctic, even with modern equipment.

These explorers, from Erik the Red to Pen Hadow, each contributed to our understanding of the Arctic in different ways.

Incredible Expeditions and Their Discoveries

One of the most famous Arctic expeditions was the voyage of the HMS Resolute, a British ship that set sail in the mid-1800s to search for Sir John Franklin and his crew. Franklin's tragic journey, which ended with both his ships trapped in the ice and his crew lost, had become a major mystery. Many countries and explorers wanted to know what had happened. The HMS Resolute was one of several ships sent to find answers. After facing dangerous ice, severe cold, and long months of isolation, the HMS Resolute itself became trapped in the ice and had to be abandoned by its crew. Amazingly, though, the story of the Resolute didn't end there. Two years later, it was found drifting in the Arctic by an American whaling ship, still largely intact. The United States returned the Resolute to Britain, and the ship was turned into a symbol of friendship between the two countries. Even today, parts of the Resolute are preserved as desks in famous places like the White House.

Another remarkable Arctic expedition was led by Roald Amundsen, a Norwegian explorer who had spent years studying how to survive in polar conditions. In 1903, Amundsen set out to find the elusive Northwest Passage, a route through the Arctic that many explorers before him had failed to navigate. Unlike earlier explorers, Amundsen knew that he couldn't rely on sheer luck or strength to make it through the ice. Instead, he took a different approach. He studied Inuit survival techniques, learning how they used dog sleds to travel across the ice and fur clothing to stay warm. These skills made a huge difference, and after spending three winters in the Arctic, Amundsen and his crew finally completed the Northwest Passage. This was a massive achievement – they had done what no one else could, and they did it by respecting and learning from the Arctic's Indigenous people.

Amundsen's success encouraged other explorers to push further into the Arctic. Just a few years later, another incredible expedition set out, this time with the goal of reaching the North Pole itself. Led by American explorer Robert Peary, this journey would go down in history. Peary's team included Matthew Henson, an African American explorer and skilled navigator, and a group of Inuit guides who provided invaluable knowledge about the Arctic. After facing bitter cold, exhausting conditions, and dangerous ice, Peary claimed to have reached the North Pole in 1909. Henson, who was by Peary's side, later said he was the first person to step onto the pole. Whether or not Peary's team truly reached the North Pole has been debated for years, but their journey was still an amazing feat, showing the world just how determined and resourceful Arctic explorers could be.

While Peary's expedition focused on reaching the North Pole, others were drawn to the Arctic for its scientific mysteries. One such expedition was led by the German scientist Alfred Wegener in the early 1900s. Wegener was fascinated by the ice and wanted to understand how the Arctic environment worked. He was especially interested in glaciers – massive, slow-moving rivers of ice that cover huge parts of the Arctic. Wegener and his team spent months on the Greenland ice sheet, conducting research that would later help scientists understand how glaciers form, move, and shape the land around them. Their discoveries helped build the foundations of glaciology, the study of glaciers, which is still an important science today. Although Wegener tragically lost his life in the Arctic, his work inspired future generations of scientists to study this icy frontier.

Not all incredible Arctic expeditions were successful, but even the failures led to important discoveries. Take, for example, the Karluk expedition of 1913. This Canadian expedition set out to explore the Arctic, but soon after entering the ice, their ship, the Karluk, became trapped and was eventually crushed. The crew, led by Captain Robert Bartlett, found themselves stranded on the ice, hundreds of miles from help. They built makeshift shelters, hunted seals and other animals for food, and did everything they could to survive. Bartlett himself set out on an epic journey across the ice to find rescue. Miraculously, after months of hardship, most of the crew survived. Although the expedition didn't accomplish its original goal, it provided valuable lessons in survival and the harsh realities of the Arctic.

In the 20th century, as technology advanced, so did Arctic expeditions. Explorers and scientists began using new tools, like airplanes and submarines, to study parts of the Arctic that were previously unreachable. One famous expedition during this time was led by Richard Byrd, an American aviator who had a fascination with the polar regions. In 1926, Byrd flew over the North Pole, giving people a bird's-eye view of this icy wilderness for the first time. While Byrd's claim of reaching the North Pole by air has been debated, his expedition was groundbreaking, showing that new technology could be used to explore the Arctic in ways that weren't possible before.

In 1937, an extraordinary Soviet expedition pushed the limits of Arctic exploration even further. A group of Soviet scientists set up a research station called North Pole-1 on a drifting ice floe – a floating piece of sea ice. Led by Ivan Papanin, these scientists spent months drifting across the Arctic Ocean, gathering valuable information about the weather, ocean currents, and ice conditions. Living on an ice floe was risky; it could crack or melt at any time, and they were surrounded by freezing water. But North Pole-1 provided scientists with important data that helped them understand how the Arctic Ocean worked, and it proved that people could live and work in the middle of the Arctic if they were well-prepared.

Modern Arctic expeditions continue to make incredible discoveries, using advanced technology to study everything from the smallest organisms living in the ice to the impact of climate change on the Arctic environment. For instance, scientists today use submarines to explore the Arctic's underwater landscape, which includes deep trenches and strange sea creatures that have adapted to the extreme cold and darkness. These expeditions have revealed new species and shown how interconnected the Arctic's ecosystem is, with each animal and plant playing an important role in the environment.

In recent years, scientists have focused on studying how climate change is affecting the Arctic. Because the Arctic is warming faster than other parts of the world, its ice is melting at an alarming rate. Modern expeditions track this melting ice using satellites, drones, and even underwater robots. By understanding how quickly the ice is disappearing, scientists can better predict what might happen to the rest of the planet. These expeditions are helping people around the world understand why the Arctic is so important – not just for the animals and plants that live there, but for everyone on Earth.

3
LIFE IN THE COLD: ARCTIC ANIMALS AND THEIR SURVIVAL SKILLS

The polar bear is probably the most famous Arctic animal. Known as the "King of the Arctic," it's the largest land predator on Earth. Adult males can weigh as much as ten men and grow up to ten feet tall when they stand on their hind legs. With their thick, creamy-white fur, polar bears blend in perfectly with the snowy landscape, making it easier for them to sneak up on their prey. They mostly eat seals, which they hunt by waiting near breathing holes in the ice. When a seal pops up to take a breath, the polar bear strikes, using its powerful paws to catch the seal.

One of the most amazing things about polar bears is their ability to stay warm in such extreme cold. They have two layers of fur and a thick layer of fat under their skin, which helps insulate them from the freezing temperatures. Even their paws are covered in fur, which not only keeps them warm but also helps them grip the slippery ice. And did you know that a polar bear's skin is actually black? This black skin helps absorb heat from the sun, giving them an extra layer of warmth. Polar bears spend much of their lives on sea ice, hunting and traveling across this frozen terrain. But as sea ice melts due to climate change, polar bears are having to travel further and work harder to find food, putting them at risk.

Another Arctic animal with impressive survival skills is the Arctic fox. This small, clever predator is perfectly suited to life in the cold. In the winter, an Arctic fox's fur turns pure white, allowing it to blend in with the snow and sneak up on prey. When summer arrives, its fur changes to a brown or gray color, which helps it hide among the rocks and plants. This color-changing ability is a great example of how animals adapt to their environment to stay safe from predators and improve their chances of hunting successfully.

Arctic foxes have small, rounded bodies and

short legs, which help them conserve heat. Their thick fur not only keeps them warm, but it also covers the bottoms of their paws, protecting them from the ice. These foxes are known for being resourceful hunters. They eat small animals like lemmings and birds, but when food is scarce, they're not too picky – they'll scavenge leftovers from larger predators like polar bears or even eat berries, seaweed, and insects. In the winter, Arctic foxes have an incredible ability to survive on very little food, and they're known to follow polar bears, hoping to catch scraps from a bear's kill.

Another animal that plays an important role in the Arctic is the walrus. These large, blubbery creatures might look slow and lazy, but they're actually well-suited for life in the Arctic Ocean. Walruses have thick layers of blubber, or fat, which keep them warm in icy waters. They use their long, curved tusks for many things, including climbing out of the water onto the ice and even breaking breathing holes in the ice. Walruses are social animals and often gather in large groups, called herds, on the ice or beaches. They mainly eat clams and other shellfish, which they find by digging their sensitive whiskers, called vibrissae, into the sea floor.

Another ocean dweller you might meet in the Arctic is the narwhal, often called the "unicorn of the sea." Narwhals are medium-sized whales known for the long, spiral tusk that sticks out from their heads. This tusk is actually an overgrown tooth, and in some narwhals, it can grow up to ten feet long! Scientists aren't entirely sure why narwhals have these tusks, but they believe it might be used to impress mates or to sense their environment. Narwhals are excellent divers and can reach depths of nearly 5,000 feet to hunt fish, squid, and shrimp. Because they live in remote parts of the Arctic Ocean, narwhals are one of the most mysterious Arctic animals, and scientists are still learning more about them.

Moving back to the land, let's talk about the mighty caribou, also known as reindeer. Caribou are famous for their long migrations, traveling hundreds or even thousands of miles each year to find food and escape harsh weather. Their large hooves help them travel over snow and ice, acting almost like snowshoes. These hooves are also useful for digging through the snow to find lichen, a type of plant that grows on rocks and trees and serves as a primary food source for caribou. Caribou are one of the few animals that can digest lichen, thanks to special bacteria in their stomachs that break it down. In winter, they rely heavily on this food source when other plants are buried under the snow.

In the skies above, you might spot the snowy owl, a beautiful white bird with piercing yellow eyes. Snowy owls are skilled hunters and are well adapted to the Arctic's open landscapes. Unlike many other owls that hunt at night, snowy owls are active during the day, especially in the Arctic summer when it stays light all the time. They have excellent eyesight and can spot prey like lemmings and other small animals from far away. Snowy owls also have a special feather structure that makes their flight nearly silent, allowing them to swoop down on their prey without being heard.

Another iconic Arctic bird is the Arctic tern, famous for its astonishing migration. Each year, Arctic terns travel from their breeding grounds in the Arctic all the way to Antarctica and back again, covering a distance of up to 44,000 miles – the longest migration of any animal on Earth. These birds spend their summers in the Arctic, where they raise their young and take advantage of the abundant food, then head to the opposite end of the planet to enjoy the Antarctic summer. This incredible journey helps them avoid the harsh Arctic winter, and it means they experience more daylight each year than almost any other animal.

Then there's the hardy muskox, a shaggy creature that looks a bit like a prehistoric beast. Muskoxen have thick coats made up of two layers: a long, shaggy outer layer and a soft, dense inner layer called qiviut, which is one of the warmest natural fibers in the world. These layers help them stay warm even in temperatures that drop to -40 degrees Fahrenheit. Muskoxen travel in herds, which gives them protection against predators like wolves. When threatened, they form a circle with their young in the center, facing outwards to defend against attackers. Muskoxen mainly eat grasses, Arctic willows, and mosses, and they use their strong hooves to dig through the snow to find food in the winter.

Birds, Fish, and Marine Life

Underneath the icy surface of the Arctic waters lies an astonishing world filled with life. While the Arctic land is home to incredible creatures like polar bears, Arctic foxes, and snowy owls, the ocean here holds secrets of its own. Arctic seas might seem dark, cold, and empty at first glance, but these waters are teeming with fish, birds, and other marine animals that have mastered the art of survival in a place most of us would consider too harsh to handle. Let's dive in and meet some of the remarkable animals that call these frigid waters home.

One of the most well-known birds of the Arctic is the puffin, often called the "clown of the sea" because of its brightly colored beak and comical appearance. Puffins are excellent divers, using their wings like flippers to swim through the water in search of fish, their main food source. They can dive as deep as 200 feet, which is pretty impressive for a small bird! Puffins have special waterproof feathers that keep them warm and dry, even in icy waters. They build nests in burrows on cliffs along the Arctic coastline, and every year, they return to the same spot to raise their chicks. During the winter, puffins' colorful beaks fade to a duller shade, making them harder to spot in the water, and their bright colors return when it's time to attract a mate.

Another famous Arctic bird is the murre, sometimes called the "penguin of the north." While murres aren't actually related to penguins, they share some similar features. These black-and-white birds are strong, fast swimmers and can dive up to 600 feet underwater, chasing after fish and squid. Murres gather in huge colonies along rocky cliffs, often in the thousands, making their nesting sites look like a bustling city. Each pair of murres lays a single egg on the cliff ledge, and both parents take turns incubating it and protecting it from predators like gulls. Once the chick hatches, it faces a thrilling test of bravery: at only a few weeks old, the chick leaps off the cliff into the ocean below, where its parents continue to care for it until it can fend for itself.

Beneath the waves, the fish that live in Arctic waters are just as fascinating. One of the most common Arctic fish is the Arctic cod, a small but incredibly tough fish that plays a crucial role in the Arctic food chain. Arctic cod are a favorite food for many larger animals, including seals, seabirds, and even whales. To survive in the frigid waters, Arctic cod have a natural "antifreeze" protein in their blood that keeps their bodies from freezing solid. This special protein stops ice crystals from forming in their blood, allowing them to thrive in water temperatures that would kill most other fish. Arctic cod often travel in schools, which helps protect them from predators and makes it easier to find food.

Then there's the Greenland shark, one of the most mysterious and unusual fish in the Arctic Ocean. Greenland sharks are huge, reaching lengths of up to 24 feet, but what makes them especially fascinating is their age. Scientists believe that Greenland sharks can live for over 400 years, making them one of the longest-living vertebrates on Earth. Imagine a shark that could have been alive when pirates sailed the seas or even before the founding of many countries! Greenland sharks move very slowly and tend to live in deep, cold waters. They have sharp teeth and feed on a variety of prey, from fish to seals. Because they live in such remote, dark places, Greenland sharks are difficult to study, and scientists are still learning more about these ancient giants.

Moving further down the food chain, we find tiny creatures called zooplankton, which are a major source of food for many Arctic animals. Zooplankton are tiny, drifting organisms that include small shrimp-like creatures, jellyfish, and fish larvae. While they may be small, zooplankton are crucial to the Arctic ecosystem. These little creatures feed on even tinier plants called phytoplankton, which use sunlight to make their food through photosynthesis. In the summer, when the Arctic gets 24 hours of daylight, phytoplankton bloom in massive numbers, creating a feast for zooplankton. This, in turn, attracts fish, birds, and whales, all eager to enjoy the seasonal abundance.

One of the most awe-inspiring animals that relies on zooplankton is the bowhead whale. These massive whales are perfectly suited for life in icy waters, with thick blubber layers that insulate them from the cold. Bowhead whales are unique in several ways. For one, they have enormous heads with thick skulls that allow them to break through sea ice to breathe. This skill is essential for living in an environment where much of the surface is frozen. Bowhead whales also have the largest mouths of any animal, which they use to filter huge amounts of water in search of tiny prey. Like the Greenland shark, bowhead whales are believed to have incredibly long lifespans, with some living well over 200 years.

Another giant of the Arctic Ocean is the beluga whale, known for its bright white color and friendly appearance. Belugas are social animals that travel in groups called pods and communicate using a variety of sounds, including whistles, clicks, and even chirps, earning them the nickname "canaries of the sea." They have flexible necks, which allow them to turn their heads in different directions – a unique trait among whales. Belugas rely on their keen sense of hearing and echolocation (a natural sonar) to navigate through the dark, icy waters and find food.

They feed on fish, squid, and crustaceans, and during the winter, they sometimes become trapped in areas surrounded by ice, where they must find small breathing holes to survive until the ice melts.

While fish and whales dominate the Arctic Ocean, there are also smaller, colorful creatures like sea anemones and starfish that live on the ocean floor. These creatures may seem out of place in such a cold environment, but they have found ways to adapt to the low temperatures and reduced light. Arctic sea anemones, for instance, anchor themselves to rocks and capture tiny particles of food drifting by in the water. Starfish, meanwhile, use their many arms to move slowly across the sea floor, hunting for clams, sea snails, and other small animals. These bottom-dwelling creatures may not be as famous as polar bears or puffins, but they play an important role in the Arctic ecosystem.

One of the most unusual Arctic animals is the icefish, a type of fish that lives in the freezing waters near Antarctica and in parts of the Arctic. Icefish have a unique adaptation – they don't have red blood cells. Instead, their blood is clear, allowing it to flow more easily in cold temperatures. This unique trait makes icefish more efficient in absorbing oxygen, which is essential for survival in an environment where the water holds less oxygen due to its low temperature.

How Animals Adapt to Extreme Cold

One of the biggest challenges animals face in the Arctic is staying warm. The cold can freeze skin and tissue, and without protection, animals could lose too much heat and risk death. To fight the chill, many Arctic animals have developed thick layers of fur, feathers, or fat that work like an extra winter coat. Polar bears, for example, have two layers of fur: a dense undercoat close to the skin and a layer of guard hairs on top. These guard hairs are actually hollow, trapping heat close to the body and providing extra insulation. Polar bears also have a thick layer of blubber beneath their skin, which acts like a built-in blanket. This blubber helps them stay warm, even when they swim in the frigid Arctic Ocean.

Walruses are another animal with thick blubber, and theirs can be as much as six inches deep! This blubber keeps them warm while they dive into icy waters in search of food, and it also serves as an energy reserve when food is hard to find. Because walruses spend a lot of time lying on ice floes, their thick layer of fat protects them from the cold surface. It's like having a cozy sleeping bag around them at all times.

Birds in the Arctic have their own special ways of dealing with the cold. Take the snowy owl, for instance. Unlike many other owls that have thin feathers, snowy owls are covered in thick, fluffy feathers that trap warmth close to their bodies. Even their legs and feet are feathered, which keeps them warm while they perch on the icy ground or fly through the freezing air. These feathered "boots" help them conserve body heat, making it possible for them to hunt and fly even in bitter temperatures.

Puffins, those colorful "clowns of the sea," also have waterproof feathers that help them stay dry and warm when they dive into icy waters to catch fish. Their feathers trap a layer of air close to their bodies, acting as insulation against the cold. This means that even after a long dive, a puffin stays dry and warm on the inside, ready for another chilly plunge. Puffins, like other seabirds, will often fluff up their feathers to create more air pockets, which increases their warmth and helps them stay comfortable in the cold Arctic air.

Besides staying warm, Arctic animals also have to move through the snow and ice, often covering long distances to find food. Some animals have developed special body parts that act like built-in snowshoes or ice grips. Caribou, for instance, have large, wide hooves that spread out their weight, allowing them to walk on top of the snow instead of sinking into it. These hooves are also sharp and strong, making it easy for caribou to dig through snow to find lichen and other plants to eat during the winter. In the summer, the hooves soften, which helps them move across the wet, boggy tundra.

Arctic foxes, with their small, compact bodies, are also built for walking on snow. Their short legs and round bodies help them conserve heat by reducing the amount of skin exposed to the cold. Their furry paws act like natural snow boots, protecting them from frostbite and giving them better grip on slippery ice. These adaptations allow the Arctic fox to hunt and explore even in the most challenging winter conditions. When food is scarce, the Arctic fox is known to follow polar bears, scavenging leftovers from their kills – a smart way to find food without much effort.

One of the most extreme adaptations to the Arctic cold can be found in fish, like the Arctic cod. Unlike mammals and birds, which need to stay warm, fish are cold-blooded and match their body temperature to the water around them. Arctic cod have a unique adaptation that prevents their blood from freezing. They produce a natural antifreeze protein that keeps ice crystals from forming in their blood and cells, allowing them to survive in temperatures that would freeze most other fish solid. This antifreeze protein helps Arctic cod and other fish thrive in the icy waters of the Arctic, where they provide a key food source for many animals, including seabirds, seals, and whales.

The Greenland shark is another fish that has adapted to survive in extreme cold. This mysterious shark moves very slowly and has a low metabolism, which means it doesn't need as much food to survive. Greenland sharks are thought to live for hundreds of years, in part because of their slow, steady lifestyle. By moving slowly and conserving energy, they can survive on a limited diet in the cold, deep waters of the Arctic, making the most of their surroundings without needing much warmth or light.

Some Arctic animals adapt to the cold by changing their behavior during different seasons. For example, the Arctic tern, a small but mighty bird, avoids the Arctic winter by migrating all the way to Antarctica, covering up to 44,000 miles in a round trip every year. This means that the Arctic tern experiences more daylight than any other creature on Earth, spending summers in the Arctic and then escaping the harsh winter by flying south to warmer waters. This remarkable journey allows the Arctic tern to thrive without facing the extreme cold all year round.

Hibernation and torpor are also strategies used by some animals to survive the winter. While true hibernation is rare in the Arctic, some animals, like the Arctic ground squirrel, enter a state of deep sleep during the winter, lowering their body temperature and slowing their metabolism to conserve energy. This allows them to survive for months without food, using up the fat reserves they built up during the summer. When spring arrives, they wake up, ready to find food and start the cycle again. The Arctic ground squirrel is one of the few mammals that can actually lower its body temperature below freezing during hibernation – a remarkable feat that showcases how tough Arctic animals can be.

Insects in the Arctic, like the woolly bear caterpillar, have their own unique way of handling the cold. Woolly bear caterpillars freeze almost completely solid during the winter, with ice forming in their bodies and even in their cells. Special chemicals in their bodies keep the ice from damaging their tissues, and when spring arrives, the caterpillars thaw out and continue their life cycle. It can take several years for a woolly bear caterpillar to become a moth, as they spend each winter in this frozen state, waiting for the brief Arctic summer to come around.

4

THE PEOPLE OF THE ARCTIC

The Arctic isn't just home to incredible animals and freezing landscapes; it's also home to resilient people who have lived there for thousands of years. These are the Indigenous tribes of the Arctic, such as the Inuit, Sami, Chukchi, and others. They've adapted to this harsh environment, developing unique ways of life and creating rich cultures that continue to thrive. Living in such a challenging place requires not only survival skills but also a deep connection to the land, animals, and seasons.

One of the largest and best-known Arctic Indigenous groups is the Inuit, who live across northern Canada, Greenland, Alaska, and parts of Siberia. The word "Inuit" means "the people" in their language, Inuktitut, and it's a fitting name for a group that has such a strong sense of community. Life in the Arctic has always been about working together, and the Inuit rely on their families and communities to survive. Each member has a role to play, from hunting and fishing to sewing clothes and building homes. Knowledge and skills are passed down from generation to generation, and every person learns the traditions that help them survive in this unique land.

Inuit homes were traditionally built from materials that were readily available in the Arctic environment, such as snow, ice, and animal hides. During the winter, they constructed igloos, which are dome-shaped shelters made from blocks of packed snow. Igloos might look simple, but they're actually an ingenious way to stay warm. Snow is an excellent insulator, trapping heat inside the igloo. A small fire or even body heat can make the inside of an igloo much warmer than the outside. In the summer, when the snow melts, the Inuit often use tents made from animal skins stretched over a wooden or bone frame. These tents are lightweight and can be easily moved, allowing the Inuit to follow the animals they hunt.

Hunting has always been central to Inuit life. In a

land where plants are scarce, animals provide food, clothing, and tools. The Inuit traditionally hunt seals, whales, caribou, and fish, depending on the season. Hunting isn't just about survival; it's a skill passed down through generations, and it teaches patience, respect for animals, and an understanding of the environment. Seals, for instance, are a major source of food, and Inuit hunters wait by breathing holes in the ice, sometimes for hours, for a seal to surface. This kind of hunting requires deep knowledge of animal behavior, ice conditions, and patience, skills that young Inuit learn from their elders.

Another Arctic group with a long history is the Sami, who live in northern Scandinavia, across Norway, Sweden, Finland, and parts of Russia. The Sami have lived in this region for thousands of years and have a culture that is closely tied to reindeer herding. Reindeer are central to Sami life, providing food, clothing, and a means of transportation. The Sami people are skilled herders, guiding their reindeer across vast stretches of land to find grazing grounds. They know the land deeply, understanding the movement of the reindeer, the changes in weather, and the cycles of the seasons.

The Sami people have their own language and

rich cultural traditions, including music, art, and clothing. One unique part of Sami culture is the joik, a traditional form of singing that is more than just music – it's a way of expressing a person, animal, or place through song. A joik doesn't tell a story or have lyrics like most songs; instead, it captures the spirit or essence of something. Sami people use joiking to honor family members, celebrate special moments, and express their connection to the natural world. It's a beautiful reminder of how deeply the Sami are connected to their surroundings.

Just as the Inuit rely on their knowledge of the land and animals to survive, the Sami have adapted to the Arctic in ways that make the most of their environment. Their clothing, for example, is designed to keep them warm during long, cold winters. Traditional Sami clothing, called gákti, is made from reindeer hide and decorated with bright colors and patterns. Each gákti is unique, often reflecting the family or community it comes from, and it serves both practical and cultural purposes. The gákti is durable, warm, and suited to the Arctic climate, while also showing pride in Sami identity.

Across the Bering Strait in Russia, you'll find another group of Arctic people known as the Chukchi. The Chukchi live in Siberia's far northeast and have a culture centered around herding reindeer and hunting marine animals like seals and whales. Chukchi hunters are skilled at navigating icy waters, often using kayaks, small boats made from animal skins stretched over a wooden frame, to hunt seals and walruses. Like the Inuit, the Chukchi have a close relationship with the sea and the animals that live there. They view hunting as a sacred act and believe that animals offer themselves to the hunters, who must show respect in return.

The Chukchi also have a fascinating spiritual tradition that involves shamanism, a belief in spirits that inhabit the natural world. Shamans are community leaders who can communicate with these spirits, offering guidance, healing, and wisdom. Through rituals, dances, and songs, shamans connect with the spiritual realm, bringing their community closer to the natural world. In a land where life is closely tied to nature's rhythms, the Chukchi's spiritual beliefs are an important part of understanding their connection to the Arctic.

Although these groups live far apart, they share many similarities. The Arctic's Indigenous people have developed unique ways to survive and thrive in one of the most extreme environments on Earth. They know how to make warm clothing, build sturdy shelters, and find food in places that seem barren. But perhaps even more importantly, they have a deep respect for the land, animals, and seasons. Their cultures have evolved in harmony with nature, and they understand that survival depends on balance – a balance between taking what they need and giving back to the land.

For the Arctic's Indigenous people, traditions aren't just things of the past; they're a living part of everyday life. From hunting techniques to language to spiritual practices, these traditions are passed down through generations, keeping the wisdom of the ancestors alive. Elders play a crucial role in teaching young people about their culture, sharing stories, and guiding them as they learn the skills needed to survive. These stories often include legends about animals, heroes, and spirits, showing the connection between people and nature. For example, the Inuit have legends about the northern lights, known as "aurora borealis," which are said to be the spirits of ancestors dancing in the sky.

Traditional Lifestyles and Cultures

Living in the Arctic isn't just about surviving the cold; it's about creating a whole way of life that's perfectly suited to the environment. For thousands of years, the Indigenous people of the Arctic – the Inuit, Sami, Chukchi, and others – have developed lifestyles and cultures that are deeply connected to the land, sea, and animals around them. These traditional ways of life go beyond just getting through the winter; they involve art, storytelling, rituals, and skills that have been passed down through generations, each step rooted in respect for the Arctic environment.

One of the most important aspects of Arctic life is knowing how to use what nature provides. For example, the Inuit have long relied on the animals they hunt, not just for food, but for almost every part of their daily lives. A seal hunt provides meat for eating, blubber for fuel, and skin for clothing. Seal bones might be used to make tools, while the sinew (tough fibers from the animal) can be used as thread. Nothing goes to waste. This tradition of using every part of an animal shows a deep respect for the resources around them and a commitment to sustainability, a practice long before it became a popular word.

The Sami people, known for their reindeer herding, also make use of every part of the reindeer. Reindeer are central to Sami life, and they provide food, clothing, and even transportation. Sami clothing, called gákti, is often made from reindeer hide and decorated with bright colors and patterns. Each piece of gákti is unique, often symbolizing the region or family that the wearer comes from. Gákti isn't just practical, though; it's a way for the Sami to express pride in their culture and identity. The patterns and colors reflect Sami traditions, telling a story about who they are and where they come from.

In addition to clothing, Arctic communities have unique methods for building shelter. The Inuit, for instance, are famous for their igloos, but not everyone knows how ingenious these structures really are. Made from blocks of packed snow, igloos are built in a dome shape, which makes them incredibly strong. Snow might seem like a strange choice for building material, but it's actually a great insulator. Inside an igloo, the temperature can be surprisingly warm, especially when compared to the frigid air outside. Sometimes, a small fire or even body heat is enough to keep an igloo comfortable. The Inuit build igloos in a specific way, carefully placing each block and leaving a small hole at the top to allow smoke to escape.

In the warmer months, when igloos aren't practical, many Arctic people use tents made from animal hides stretched over a frame. These tents are portable, lightweight, and durable – perfect for a lifestyle that involves moving with the seasons to follow animal migrations. Both the Sami and the Chukchi people have a history of using tents, which they can quickly set up and take down. The Chukchi, who live in northeastern Siberia, use a type of tent called a yaranga. The yaranga is covered in reindeer skins and has a chimney at the top, which allows smoke from the fire to escape. Inside, layers of reindeer hide help keep the space warm and comfortable, even when the weather outside is harsh.

In every Arctic community, food isn't just something to eat; it's a central part of culture and tradition. The Inuit have a diet rich in fish, seals, caribou, and other animals. Since fruits and vegetables are hard to find in the Arctic, people here rely on hunting and fishing to get their nutrition. This high-protein, high-fat diet is perfect for staying warm and energized in the cold. Fish, especially Arctic char and salmon, are also important in Inuit and Sami diets. They are often caught in rivers or the sea and can be eaten fresh, dried, or frozen. In fact, frozen fish is a traditional Arctic delicacy, eaten raw and full of nutrients.

Hunting and fishing aren't just about gathering food – they're seen as skills and traditions that connect people to their ancestors and the natural world. Young Inuit children learn to hunt from a young age, often accompanying their parents and elders on hunting trips. They learn how to track animals, read signs in the snow, and understand the behavior of the wildlife around them. These skills aren't written down in books; they're taught through experience, passed down as part of a living tradition. Even today, many young people in Arctic communities take pride in learning these skills, which are both a part of their heritage and a way to connect with their environment.

Storytelling is another key part of Arctic culture. The Indigenous people of the Arctic tell stories that have been passed down for generations. These stories aren't just for entertainment; they teach lessons, share history, and explain the natural world. Many Inuit stories involve animals, like the raven, who is known as a trickster in Inuit mythology. The raven often plays pranks on others but also teaches important lessons about respect, honesty, and kindness. The Sami also have a rich tradition of stories, including legends about spirits that protect the land and animals. These stories are often told around fires during the long, dark winter nights, bringing families and communities together.

The Sami have a unique type of singing called joiking, which is used to honor people, animals, and places. A joik isn't like a regular song with lyrics and verses; instead, it captures the spirit or feeling of something or someone. Each joik is unique and personal, almost like a musical portrait. Joiking is a powerful way for the Sami to express their feelings and connect with the world around them. Traditionally, joiking was used in ceremonies, celebrations, and even to pass down history and stories. Today, it's still a beloved art form that keeps Sami culture alive and connects the Sami people to their roots.

For the Chukchi, who live in Russia's northeastern Siberia, spirituality and connection to nature are central to their way of life. The Chukchi believe that everything in nature has a spirit – the animals, the trees, the rivers, even the mountains. Shamans, or spiritual leaders, play an important role in Chukchi society. They act as healers, guides, and storytellers, and they help people connect with the spirits of nature. Through songs, dances, and rituals, shamans bring people together, sharing wisdom and offering guidance. The Chukchi people believe that respecting the spirits of nature is essential for a balanced life, and this belief shapes how they hunt, build, and live.

Celebrations and festivals are also important parts of life in Arctic communities. The Sami, for example, celebrate festivals throughout the year, often involving reindeer herding competitions, traditional music, and dance. During these events, people wear their best gákti, the colorful clothing that reflects their family and region. These gatherings are a time for communities to come together, to share stories, enjoy music, and celebrate their culture. The festivals are often open to outsiders as well, offering a chance to learn about Sami traditions and experience the warmth and hospitality of Arctic communities.

As modern technology and lifestyle changes reach even the most remote places, many Arctic Indigenous people are finding new ways to combine their traditional knowledge with modern life. Snowmobiles and motorboats have made hunting and travel faster, but many still prefer traditional methods, especially for cultural and ceremonial purposes. Schools in Arctic regions often teach both traditional skills and modern subjects, helping young people stay connected to their heritage while preparing them for life in a rapidly changing world.

How Arctic Communities Survive and Thrive Today

Life in the Arctic today is a unique blend of ancient traditions and modern conveniences. People in Arctic communities still rely on the land, the sea, and the wisdom of their ancestors, but they also have access to new technologies and resources that make life a little easier. While the Arctic landscape and climate haven't changed much, the way people live here has evolved, allowing them to thrive in one of the harshest environments on Earth.

For many Arctic communities, food is still gathered from the land and sea. Hunting, fishing, and gathering are essential, not just for survival but as a way to stay connected to nature and tradition. In parts of Canada and Greenland, the Inuit continue to hunt seals, caribou, and whales, just as their ancestors did. Hunting requires skill, patience, and deep knowledge of the environment. Today, however, hunters often use snowmobiles and GPS devices to navigate the vast landscape, making it safer and easier to reach distant hunting grounds.

Fishing is another key part of Arctic life. In places like Norway and Alaska, fishing has become a major industry, providing jobs and food for local communities and beyond. While traditional fishing methods are still used, many fishers today rely on modern boats, equipment, and processing facilities to catch and prepare fish. Arctic char, cod, and salmon are some of the region's main catches, and they're sold not only locally but also exported around the world. For Arctic communities, fishing isn't just a way to make a living; it's a way to maintain a close connection to the ocean and the life it supports.

Reindeer herding is an important part of life for the Sami people of northern Scandinavia. Reindeer have been at the center of Sami culture for centuries, providing food, clothing, and transportation. Today, reindeer herding is a blend of tradition and technology. Sami herders still guide their reindeer across the tundra, following seasonal migrations, but they also use snowmobiles, GPS, and even drones to track and manage their herds. These tools help herders keep their reindeer safe and make it easier to cover the vast distances needed to find food for the animals. Reindeer herding remains a family activity, with knowledge and skills passed down from one generation to the next, keeping this ancient way of life alive in a modern world.

While traditional practices are still strong, Arctic

communities have also adapted to modern life in other ways. Houses in the Arctic are built to withstand extreme cold and heavy snowfall. Many homes have extra insulation, triple-paned windows, and strong roofs to keep the warmth in and the snow out. In areas with permafrost (permanently frozen ground), buildings are often raised on stilts to prevent the heat from the building from melting the ground underneath. This keeps the houses stable and prevents them from sinking into the softening earth as the Arctic climate changes.

Schools in the Arctic teach both modern subjects and traditional skills. Children learn math, science, and history, just like students anywhere else, but they also have the chance to learn traditional crafts, hunting techniques, and language. For example, in Inuit communities, children might learn how to sew parkas, make tools from animal bones, or navigate by reading the snow and ice. Sami schools often teach the Sami language, joiking (a form of singing), and the skills needed for reindeer herding. This combination of old and new knowledge gives young people a well-rounded education that connects them to their heritage and prepares them for the future.

Healthcare in the Arctic has also improved with

modern advancements. In remote communities, people used to rely on traditional healers and home remedies, but today, many Arctic towns have clinics and hospitals with doctors and nurses who provide medical care. In the most isolated areas, medical professionals can visit patients by plane or helicopter, and telemedicine allows doctors to consult with patients over video calls. However, traditional knowledge is still respected, and some people combine modern medicine with traditional practices to stay healthy.

Arctic communities are also finding ways to use renewable energy, such as wind and solar power. The Arctic gets plenty of sunlight during the summer months, and many communities have begun to install solar panels on buildings to harness this energy. Wind power is also becoming popular in areas with strong winds. These renewable energy sources help reduce the use of imported fuel, which can be expensive and difficult to transport to remote areas. By using the natural resources around them, Arctic communities are working to become more self-sufficient and environmentally friendly.

Climate change is one of the biggest challenges facing Arctic communities today. Rising temperatures are causing the sea ice to melt, and the permafrost to thaw, and are changing animal migration patterns. These changes have a big impact on people's lives, making hunting and fishing more difficult and affecting the stability of buildings and roads. Indigenous leaders and scientists are working together to monitor these changes and find ways to adapt. Traditional knowledge, like understanding animal behavior and weather patterns, combined with scientific data, helps communities prepare for an uncertain future.

One way Arctic communities are addressing climate change is by sharing their stories and knowledge with the world. Indigenous leaders often attend international meetings and speak about the changes they're seeing in their homelands. Through these conversations, they hope to encourage global action to protect the Arctic and reduce climate change's impact. By combining traditional knowledge with modern science, Arctic communities are making their voices heard, reminding everyone that the Arctic is a vital part of the world that needs to be protected.

Arctic communities are also opening their doors to visitors, welcoming people who want to learn more about their cultures and landscapes. Tourism in the Arctic has become more popular, with people traveling from around the world to see the northern lights, experience dog sledding, and learn about Indigenous cultures. For Arctic communities, tourism provides jobs and an opportunity to share their traditions and stories with others. However, they are also careful to protect their land and culture from the negative effects of too many visitors. By managing tourism carefully, Arctic people are finding ways to balance tradition and modern opportunities.

5

ICE AND SNOW

Glaciers are one of the Arctic's most impressive natural features. These massive rivers of ice are created from layer upon layer of compacted snow, slowly building up over thousands of years. Picture a mountain valley filled with snow, where each snowfall adds another layer. Over time, as the snow piles up, the pressure causes it to compress and turn into solid ice. When this ice becomes thick and heavy enough, it starts to flow very slowly downhill, forming a glacier. Even though glaciers move at a snail's pace, they're incredibly powerful, grinding down rocks and carving valleys as they go. In fact, many of the Arctic's valleys and fjords were carved by glaciers thousands of years ago.

One of the fascinating things about glaciers is that they're always moving. Even though they seem still and solid, the ice is actually flowing, like a frozen river. Some glaciers move only a few inches a year, while others can flow up to several feet. The movement of glaciers shapes the landscape around them, creating steep cliffs, ridges, and deep valleys. This slow movement also creates crevasses, deep cracks in the glacier that can be very dangerous. These crevasses can be hidden by snow, making it risky for hikers or researchers who cross the glacier's surface.

When a glacier reaches the edge of the land and touches the ocean, something incredible happens: pieces of the glacier break off and float away, forming icebergs. Icebergs are like giant, floating mountains of ice, and they can be as big as a small town. Most of an iceberg's mass is actually underwater – only about 10% sticks up above the surface, which is why ships have to be careful when they're near one. The part of an iceberg that's below the water is much bigger and can be unpredictable. Icebergs drift with ocean currents, moving wherever the sea takes them, and they can travel far from the Arctic.

The colors of an iceberg are also something to

admire. They aren't just plain white – many icebergs have shades of blue, green, and even stripes. The blue color comes from the way ice absorbs light. In ice that's packed tightly, like glacier ice, only blue light can pass through, which gives the iceberg its stunning color. Sometimes, you'll see green or even black stripes in an iceberg. These colors come from different layers of snow, dust, and minerals that were frozen into the glacier as it formed.

While icebergs are large and dramatic, sea ice is a bit different. Sea ice forms when the surface of the ocean itself freezes, creating a layer of ice that floats on top of the water. Unlike glaciers, which are made from fresh water, sea ice is salty, just like the ocean. This saltiness makes sea ice a bit softer and less dense than glacier ice, and it's often thinner. Sea ice usually forms in the winter, when temperatures drop low enough to freeze the ocean's surface, and it melts back again in the summer. In some parts of the Arctic, however, sea ice stays frozen year-round, creating a permanent icy landscape.

Sea ice plays a crucial role in the Arctic ecosystem. It provides a habitat for animals like polar bears, seals, and walruses, which depend on it for hunting, resting, and raising their young. Polar bears, for example, use sea ice as a platform to hunt seals. They roam across the ice, using their keen sense of smell to detect seals that come up for air through breathing holes. Sea ice also offers protection to seals and walruses, who rest on the ice and dive into the water if they sense danger. Without sea ice, many Arctic animals would struggle to survive.

The ice in the Arctic does more than just provide a home for animals; it also has a big impact on the Earth's climate. Ice reflects sunlight, which helps keep the Arctic cool. When sunlight hits the white surface of sea ice, it bounces back into space, preventing the Arctic from heating up too much. This reflection of sunlight is called the albedo effect, and it's one of the reasons why the Arctic stays cold. But as the climate changes and more sea ice melts, there's less ice to reflect the sunlight, which causes the Arctic to warm up even more. This warming effect has a ripple effect across the globe, influencing weather patterns and temperatures far beyond the Arctic.

One of the places where you can see the effects of melting sea ice is along the Northwest Passage, a route through the Arctic Ocean that connects the Atlantic and Pacific Oceans. For centuries, explorers searched for a way through this icy maze, hoping it would provide a shortcut for ships traveling between

Europe and Asia. In the past, the Northwest Passage was often blocked by thick sea ice, making it nearly impossible to cross. But as the Arctic warms, the sea ice in the Northwest Passage is melting, allowing ships to navigate through it more easily. This change has opened new possibilities for shipping and trade, but it also raises concerns about the impact on the Arctic environment and the animals that rely on sea ice.

The changes in the Arctic ice aren't just limited to sea ice; glaciers are also melting. As glaciers lose ice, they contribute to rising sea levels, which can affect coastlines around the world. When a glacier melts, the water flows into rivers and eventually reaches the ocean, adding more water to the seas. Scientists are carefully studying glaciers in the Arctic to understand how fast they're melting and what this means for the future. Melting glaciers can also create other changes in the Arctic landscape, such as forming new lakes and changing the flow of rivers.

The Tundra Ecosystem and Its Unique Plant Life

Stretching out across the Arctic is a vast, treeless region called the tundra. Unlike the icy seas or towering glaciers, the tundra is an open, frozen landscape with a unique ecosystem that's often overlooked. At first glance, the tundra might seem like a barren place with little to offer, but this cold, windswept land is actually full of life. Plants and animals here have found surprising ways to survive in conditions that would challenge even the hardiest species in warmer climates. Beneath the snow and frost, the tundra is a place of resilience, with plants and wildlife that contribute to the Arctic's delicate balance.

The tundra is defined by its lack of trees, a fact that makes it very different from other biomes, like forests or grasslands. The reason trees don't grow here is because of the permafrost – a layer of permanently frozen ground that lies just beneath the surface. Even during the brief Arctic summer, when the snow melts and temperatures rise, only a thin layer of soil above the permafrost thaws. This thin, soggy layer is all that plants have to work with, and it makes it difficult for larger plants with deep roots to grow. Instead, the tundra is filled with low-growing plants like mosses, grasses, and shrubs, which have adapted to these unique conditions.

Mosses are among the most common plants in the tundra. Unlike trees, mosses don't need deep roots to survive. Instead, they spread out across the ground, creating thick, spongy mats that can hold moisture. This is an important feature in the tundra, where water is often scarce. Mosses are tough and can survive extreme cold and dry conditions, making them perfect for the Arctic landscape. During the summer, they soak up the moisture from melting snow and ice, storing it for the dry winter months ahead. Mosses also provide an important habitat for small insects and serve as a soft bed for animals like caribou, who sometimes munch on moss when other food sources are limited.

Another plant that thrives in the tundra is lichen, which isn't actually a single plant but a combination of algae and fungi living together in a symbiotic relationship. This team-up allows lichen to survive in places where other plants can't. Lichens grow directly on rocks, soil, and even on tree bark in other parts of the world, absorbing nutrients from the air and rainfall. They are incredibly slow-growing, sometimes taking years to cover even a small area, but they are tough enough to endure the Arctic's freezing temperatures and strong winds. Lichen is a key food source for many Arctic animals, especially caribou and reindeer, who rely on it for energy during the winter months when other plants are scarce.

Arctic grasses are also common on the tundra. Unlike the tall, swaying grasses you might see in other parts of the world, Arctic grasses grow low to the ground. They form dense clusters, which helps protect them from the wind and cold. The leaves of these grasses are narrow, which reduces the amount of water they lose. Water is precious on the tundra, and plants here can't afford to waste any. During the short summer, these grasses burst into life, turning parts of the tundra green and providing food for grazing animals.

In addition to mosses, lichens, and grasses, the tundra is home to a surprising variety of flowering plants. Arctic poppies, for example, add spots of yellow to the landscape during the summer. These small flowers have a clever trick to help them make the most of the limited sunlight: they follow the sun as it moves across the sky. This sun-tracking behavior allows the Arctic poppy to stay warm and maximize the energy it gets from the sun. Other flowering plants on the tundra include purple saxifrage and Arctic willow, which grow low to the ground, often spreading out in clusters to trap heat and reduce wind exposure.

The Arctic willow, sometimes called the "polar willow," is one of the most remarkable plants in the tundra. Unlike willows in other parts of the world, the Arctic willow is very small, often growing no more than a few inches tall. It has adapted to the cold by growing close to the ground, where it can benefit from the slight warmth of the soil. Arctic willows also have tiny, fuzzy hairs on their leaves, which help trap heat and reduce water loss. These adaptations make the Arctic willow incredibly resilient, allowing it to survive the harsh conditions of the tundra. The plant is also an important food source for animals like Arctic hares and caribou, who munch on its leaves and twigs.

When summer arrives, the tundra undergoes an amazing transformation. The snow melts, the days become longer, and the sun shines almost 24 hours a day. This constant daylight is a boost for the plants, which have only a few short weeks to grow, flower, and produce seeds. The tundra bursts with color during this time, with wildflowers, grasses, and mosses covering the landscape. This brief but intense growing season provides food for animals like caribou, lemmings, and Arctic hares, who rely on the plants for sustenance.

Animals that live on the tundra play a big role in

shaping the ecosystem. Caribou and reindeer, for example, travel across vast distances in search of food, grazing on the mosses, lichens, and grasses of the tundra. Their migrations help spread seeds and nutrients across the land, supporting plant growth and keeping the tundra healthy. Lemmings, small rodents that dig through the snow to find plants and roots, are another important part of the tundra ecosystem. These tiny creatures are a key food source for predators like Arctic foxes, snowy owls, and even wolves.

Changes in the Arctic Climate

In the Arctic, ice isn't just a layer covering the ground – it's the foundation of life for animals, plants, and people. For thousands of years, the Arctic ice has followed a cycle of melting and freezing, with sea ice stretching across the ocean in winter and shrinking back in summer. Glaciers have rested high in the mountains, growing with each snowfall, while permafrost has kept the ground solid and stable. But in recent decades, something has changed. Scientists have noticed that the Arctic's ice isn't following the same patterns anymore. Sea ice is melting faster, glaciers are retreating, and permafrost is thawing in ways never seen before. These changes are transforming the Arctic, and their effects are reaching far beyond the polar circle.

To understand what's happening to the ice, it's helpful to look at the science behind it. The Arctic's ice acts like a giant mirror, reflecting sunlight and helping keep the region cool. This reflection is called the albedo effect, and it's one of the main reasons the Arctic stays cold. When sunlight hits the bright, white ice, much of it bounces back into space. But as the ice melts and exposes darker surfaces like the ocean or tundra, more heat is absorbed, which makes the Arctic even warmer. This process creates a loop: the more ice that melts, the warmer it gets, which causes even more ice to melt. Scientists call this a feedback loop, and it's one of the reasons why the Arctic is warming up faster than other parts of the world.

One of the biggest changes in the Arctic is happening to sea ice. Sea ice forms when the surface of the ocean freezes, creating a layer of ice that floats on the water. Each winter, the sea ice spreads out, covering millions of square miles, but it doesn't all melt away in the summer. Instead, some of the ice survives from year to year, getting thicker and stronger over time. This older, thicker ice is called multiyear ice, and it's an important part of the Arctic ecosystem. But as the climate warms, more of the sea ice is melting each summer, and there's less multiyear ice remaining. In fact, scientists have recorded a dramatic decrease in sea ice over the past few decades, with the Arctic losing an area of ice nearly the size of Texas each year.

The loss of sea ice has a big impact on Arctic animals, especially those that rely on the ice for hunting, resting, or raising their young. Polar bears, for example, use sea ice as a platform to hunt seals. They roam across the ice, following the seals' breathing holes and waiting patiently for a chance to catch their prey. As sea ice shrinks, polar bears have to travel farther to find food, and some are even swimming for miles in search of ice. This extra effort takes a toll on the bears, making it harder for them to survive and find enough food to support their cubs. Walruses, too, are affected by the shrinking ice. These massive animals rest on the ice between dives, using it as a safe platform to care for their young. Without enough sea ice, walruses have started gathering on beaches, where overcrowding can lead to dangerous situations.

It's not just animals that are feeling the effects of the melting ice. Indigenous communities in the

Arctic have long relied on sea ice for hunting and travel. When the ice is stable, people can use it as a pathway to reach hunting grounds, fishing spots, and neighboring villages. But with the ice becoming less predictable, traditional ways of life are changing. Hunters may have to travel farther to find game, and some areas that were once accessible by dog sled or snowmobile are no longer safe. For these communities, the loss of sea ice isn't just a change in the landscape; it's a shift in culture, affecting how they live, work, and connect with their environment.

Glaciers are also transforming as the Arctic warms. These massive rivers of ice have been a part of the Arctic landscape for thousands of years, shaping valleys and feeding rivers as they slowly move down mountainsides. Glaciers are formed from layers of snow that have compacted into ice over time, growing thicker with each snowfall. But as temperatures rise, many Arctic glaciers are shrinking, losing more ice in the summer than they gain in the winter. This melting doesn't just affect the Arctic; it contributes to rising sea levels around the world. As glaciers melt, the water flows into rivers and eventually reaches the ocean, adding to the volume of water in the sea. Scientists are keeping a close eye on Arctic glaciers, studying how quickly they're melting and what it means for future sea levels.

Thawing permafrost is another major change happening in the Arctic. Permafrost is a layer of frozen soil that lies just beneath the surface and can reach depths of hundreds of feet. It's like a frozen foundation that keeps the Arctic landscape stable, supporting buildings, roads, and ecosystems. But as the Arctic warms, this frozen ground is beginning to thaw, causing big changes. In some areas, the ground becomes soft and unstable when the permafrost melts, leading to cracks, sinkholes, and landslides. Buildings and roads can become damaged as the ground shifts, creating challenges for Arctic communities.

The thawing of permafrost also releases gases like carbon dioxide and methane, which have been trapped in the frozen soil for thousands of years. Both of these gases are greenhouse gases, which means they trap heat in the atmosphere and contribute to global warming. Methane, in particular, is much more powerful than carbon dioxide when it comes to warming the planet. As the permafrost thaws and releases these gases, it adds to the warming effect, creating another feedback loop that accelerates climate change.

Changes in the Arctic don't just stay in the Arctic. The warming of this region has ripple effects that reach across the globe, influencing weather patterns, ocean currents, and even the types of plants and animals that can survive in different areas. The Arctic plays a key role in regulating Earth's climate, and as it changes, scientists are working to understand what these changes mean for the planet as a whole.

To track what's happening in the Arctic, scientists use a combination of satellites, icebreakers, and research stations. Satellites orbiting the Earth can measure the extent of sea ice, the temperature of the ocean, and the movement of glaciers, providing a big-picture view of the Arctic. Icebreakers, which are powerful ships designed to cut through ice, allow scientists to explore areas that are otherwise hard to reach. At research stations in places like Greenland and Alaska, scientists collect samples of ice, soil, and air, studying everything from greenhouse gas levels to ice core records that reveal clues about past climates.

Even though the changes in the Arctic may seem overwhelming, there are people and communities working to protect this fragile environment. Indigenous leaders, scientists, and environmental groups are raising awareness about the importance of the Arctic and the need to take action on climate change. By sharing their knowledge and experiences, they're encouraging people around the world to understand that the Arctic is more than just a frozen wilderness – it's a crucial part of our planet's climate system.

6

SCIENCE IN THE ARCTIC

In the middle of the Arctic's icy landscape, surrounded by snow-covered mountains, frozen seas, and stretches of tundra, you'll find places that seem out of place at first glance: Arctic research stations. These are not just ordinary buildings but centers of discovery where scientists from around the world gather to study one of the most mysterious and important parts of our planet. In these stations, scientists brave the extreme cold, work long hours in constant daylight or darkness, and use all kinds of special tools to unlock the secrets of the Arctic. Their work helps us understand not only what's happening in the Arctic but also how it affects the entire Earth.

Living and working in these stations is a challenge. In winter, temperatures can plunge to -40°F or lower, and in summer, temperatures may still hover around freezing. Scientists often need to wear thick layers of insulated clothing and boots just to go outside, and the wind can make it feel even colder. During the Arctic winter, it's dark 24 hours a day, and during the summer, the sun doesn't set. This constant light or darkness can make it hard for scientists to keep track of time, and many of them use blackout curtains or special lamps to help them sleep and stay on a regular schedule. Despite these challenges, scientists come to the Arctic to study everything from the melting ice to the animals that live here, because they know the information they gather is important for understanding our planet.

One of the main reasons scientists are drawn to the Arctic is to study climate change. The Arctic is warming faster than anywhere else on Earth, and scientists want to understand why. To do this, they collect data on temperature, wind, and ocean currents. They set up weather stations and place sensors in the ground, in the sea, and even in the ice itself. These sensors can track temperature changes over time, helping scientists learn how quickly the Arctic is warming and what might happen in the future. Some stations even send up weather balloons, which carry instruments high into the sky to measure temperature and wind patterns. The data from these balloons helps scientists predict weather patterns not just in the Arctic but around the world.

Another key focus of Arctic research is studying sea ice. Scientists track the size and thickness of the ice, taking measurements in person or using satellite images from space. Satellite images give scientists a big-picture view of the Arctic, showing them how much ice is covering the ocean and how that amount changes with each season. But to get a closer look, researchers often need to go out onto the ice itself. They drill holes and place special tools called ice buoys, which can measure the ice's thickness and movement. By studying sea ice, scientists can learn how it affects ocean currents, weather patterns, and the animals that rely on it, like polar bears and seals.

Glaciers are another big part of Arctic research. These massive rivers of ice hold clues about Earth's history and future. Scientists drill deep into glaciers to extract ice cores – long, cylindrical samples of ice that contain trapped bubbles of air from thousands of years ago. By analyzing the air in these bubbles, scientists can learn what the atmosphere was like in the past. They can see changes in carbon dioxide levels, temperature, and even volcanic eruptions.

This information helps scientists understand how Earth's climate has changed over time and what might be in store for the future.

Permafrost, the frozen layer of ground beneath the surface, is also a focus for scientists. As the Arctic warms, this permafrost is starting to thaw, releasing greenhouse gases like carbon dioxide and methane. To study this, scientists dig into the ground and take soil samples, which they analyze to see how much carbon is stored in the permafrost. They also monitor the amount of methane being released, because methane is a powerful greenhouse gas that contributes to global warming. Understanding permafrost is crucial because as it thaws, it could speed up climate change, affecting the whole planet.

The Arctic isn't just important for its ice and permafrost – it's also home to a unique ecosystem. Scientists at Arctic research stations study the plants and animals that survive in this extreme environment. They observe polar bears, Arctic foxes, snowy owls, and other animals, tracking their movements and behavior to see how they're adapting to the changing climate. For instance, they might attach small trackers to polar bears or Arctic foxes, allowing them to follow the animals' movements over time. This information helps scientists understand how animals are coping with the shrinking sea ice and changing seasons.

Arctic researchers also study smaller creatures, like plankton and fish, that live in the icy waters. These tiny organisms are the base of the food web and are essential for the survival of larger animals, like seals and whales. By taking samples of seawater, scientists can examine the types and amounts of plankton, learning about the health of the Arctic Ocean. They use underwater robots, called remotely operated vehicles (ROVs), to explore parts of the ocean that are too dangerous for humans to reach. ROVs can dive deep below the ice, capturing videos and collecting samples of plants, animals, and even microbes. Studying the Arctic's underwater ecosystem helps scientists understand how changes in the ice and water temperature affect life in the ocean.

To carry out all this work, Arctic scientists often rely on teamwork and collaboration. Research stations are usually home to scientists from many different countries, who bring their own skills and knowledge. At some stations, you might find biologists studying animals, meteorologists tracking the weather, glaciologists studying glaciers, and chemists analyzing air samples. These scientists work together, sharing their findings and building a more complete picture of the Arctic and how it's changing. This collaboration is especially important because the Arctic affects the entire planet, and what happens here can influence climates and ecosystems around the world.

Sometimes, Arctic research isn't just about studying nature – it's also about working with the people who live here. Indigenous communities have lived in the Arctic for thousands of years, and their knowledge of the land is invaluable to scientists. Many researchers work alongside Indigenous people, learning about traditional hunting routes, animal behavior, and weather patterns. This local knowledge, combined with scientific research, provides a fuller understanding of the Arctic environment. Indigenous perspectives also help scientists see the changes in the Arctic not just as data points but as shifts that affect real people and cultures.

Studying Ice Cores, Weather, and Wildlife

One of the most powerful ways scientists study the Arctic's past is by drilling into glaciers and extracting ice cores. Imagine a huge straw that's used to dig deep into a glacier, pulling out a long, frozen cylinder of ice. This ice core is like a time capsule, preserving air bubbles, dust, and even chemicals from thousands of years ago. Each layer of ice represents a year, just like rings on a tree, and by examining these layers, scientists can travel back in time. They can learn about past climates, see how temperatures have changed over thousands of years, and even detect major events like volcanic eruptions or periods of high pollution.

To study an ice core, scientists carefully slice it into sections, taking great care to keep it frozen until it reaches a lab. In the lab, they analyze the gases trapped in the ice, looking closely at carbon dioxide, methane, and other greenhouse gases. Higher levels of these gases often indicate warmer periods in Earth's history, while lower levels suggest colder times. By comparing these levels to modern-day readings, scientists can see how human activity is impacting the climate. This work requires patience, precision, and advanced technology, but the results offer a window into the history of our atmosphere and how it might change in the future.

While ice cores reveal the Arctic's past, weather stations and satellites are helping scientists monitor the present. All across the Arctic, scientists have set up weather stations that track temperature, humidity, wind speed, and other key details. Some of these stations are located on land, while others are set up on drifting ice floes or even attached to buoys in the sea. These stations gather data constantly, sending it back to researchers who analyze the information to understand current weather patterns. By watching these changes over time, scientists can make better predictions about the Arctic's future.

Satellites play an important role in Arctic weather studies too. From high above the Earth, satellites can capture images of the entire Arctic region, showing scientists exactly where the sea ice is and how it's changing. This bird's-eye view is incredibly valuable, as it allows scientists to see areas that are too difficult or dangerous to reach on the ground. Satellite images also help scientists track the movement of large icebergs, monitor glacier changes, and measure sea surface temperatures. This data helps us understand how the Arctic influences global weather patterns, from cold fronts in North America to heat waves in Europe.

Weather stations and satellites don't just tell us about temperature and wind – they help scientists understand how the Arctic environment impacts the rest of the world. For example, changes in Arctic weather can influence ocean currents, which in turn affect temperatures and storm patterns in faraway places. The Arctic is often called the "planet's refrigerator" because it helps keep global temperatures stable. When the Arctic warms, it affects the entire climate system, creating ripple effects that reach every corner of the globe. This is one of the reasons scientists are so focused on understanding Arctic weather; they know that what happens in the Arctic doesn't stay in the Arctic.

While monitoring ice and weather gives us valuable information, understanding Arctic wildlife helps scientists see the effects of climate change up close. The Arctic is home to unique animals like polar bears, Arctic foxes, walruses, and migratory birds, all of which have adapted to survive in this cold environment. But as the climate changes, many of these animals face new challenges, and scientists are keen to study how they're adapting. To track Arctic animals, scientists use various tools, from GPS collars to drones, each providing a different type of data.

Polar bears, for example, are a focus of many Arctic research projects. Polar bears rely on sea ice to hunt seals, their primary food source. With sea ice melting earlier in the year and freezing later, polar bears have to travel greater distances to find food, which can lead to exhaustion and even starvation. To understand how polar bears are coping, scientists sometimes attach GPS collars to the bears, which track their movements across the ice. These collars allow scientists to see where the bears are going, how far they're traveling, and whether they're able to find enough food. The data collected from these collars helps scientists predict how polar bears might fare if the ice continues to shrink.

Arctic foxes are another animal that scientists study closely. These small, clever foxes have thick fur that keeps them warm even in freezing temperatures, and they're known for their resourcefulness in finding food. Scientists track Arctic foxes using small GPS devices, observing how their hunting habits and territories change with the seasons. Arctic foxes are also an important part of the food chain, as they help control the populations of small animals like lemmings and birds. By studying the movements and behavior of Arctic foxes, scientists gain insight into the health of the entire ecosystem.

Walruses, which rely on sea ice as a resting spot between feeding dives, are also feeling the effects of climate change. With less sea ice, walruses are forced to rest on land, sometimes crowding together in large numbers. This can lead to dangerous situations, especially for young walruses, who are at risk of being trampled in the crowded space. Scientists observe walrus populations to monitor their health and behavior, noting how changes in sea ice impact their feeding and breeding habits. By studying walruses, scientists learn more about the relationship between Arctic animals and their icy habitat.

In addition to large animals, scientists also study smaller creatures, such as plankton and fish, which are vital to the Arctic food chain. Plankton, tiny organisms that float in the ocean, are the foundation of the food web, supporting everything from small fish to large whales. Plankton blooms are influenced by temperature and sunlight, and as the Arctic warms, these blooms are shifting. By collecting samples of plankton and studying their populations, scientists can see how changes in the Arctic climate are affecting the entire ecosystem. Fish, too, are an important part of Arctic research, as they provide food for both wildlife and human communities. Changes in fish populations can indicate shifts in ocean conditions, helping scientists track the health of Arctic waters.

All of this work – from drilling ice cores to

tracking polar bears – is like piecing together a giant puzzle. Each discovery adds a new piece, helping scientists understand how the Arctic works and how it's changing. These studies don't just tell us about the Arctic itself; they reveal clues about the future of our planet. The Arctic may be remote, but the information gathered here is valuable for people everywhere, showing us how connected we all are to this unique and fragile environment.

What Arctic Research Tells Us About Our Planet

One of the most powerful things we learn from studying the Arctic is how interconnected everything on Earth is. The Arctic's icy landscape, which might seem far removed from daily life in warmer places, plays a big role in balancing the planet's temperature. The bright, reflective surface of sea ice and snow bounces sunlight back into space, keeping the Arctic cooler and slowing down global warming. This reflection, known as the albedo effect, helps prevent our planet from overheating. But as temperatures rise and more ice melts, less sunlight gets reflected, and more heat is absorbed by the ocean, which in turn speeds up the melting. This change doesn't just warm the Arctic; it adds to the warming of Earth as a whole.

When scientists study this melting ice, they learn about a feedback loop: a process where one change leads to another, which then circles back to intensify the original change. In the Arctic, as the ice melts, it leads to more warming, which then causes even more ice to melt. This loop has big consequences. It's like a chain reaction where one small shift sets off another, which keeps going. By studying these feedback loops in the Arctic, scientists gain a better understanding of how interconnected systems work all over the world.

Rising sea levels are another issue connected to Arctic research. When glaciers melt, the water flows into rivers and then into the ocean, slowly adding more water to the sea. Scientists track glacier melt in the Arctic to understand how fast these changes are happening. Rising sea levels might seem like a distant problem for people who live far from the coast, but they're a major concern for millions of people who live in coastal areas around the world. As sea levels rise, they increase the risk of flooding in cities, towns, and even small island nations. By studying how quickly Arctic glaciers are melting, scientists can make predictions about future sea levels, helping communities prepare and adapt.

Ocean currents are another part of Earth's system that is influenced by the Arctic. Imagine a giant conveyor belt that moves water around the planet. Warm water from the equator flows toward the poles, where it cools down and sinks, then flows back toward the equator, creating a cycle. This movement, known as the "ocean conveyor belt," helps distribute heat around the planet, making sure no one area gets too hot or too cold. The Arctic is a key part of this cycle because the cold water from melting ice sinks and drives the conveyor belt. However, as Arctic ice melts faster, the extra fresh water can disrupt this process, which could lead to changes in weather patterns around the world. By studying the Arctic, scientists can keep track of these changes and understand how they might affect weather far beyond the polar regions.

One surprising discovery from Arctic research is how much greenhouse gas is stored in permafrost. Permafrost is the frozen layer of ground beneath the tundra and Arctic forests, and it contains huge amounts of carbon in the form of frozen plant material. When permafrost thaws, this organic material begins to decompose, releasing carbon dioxide and methane into the atmosphere. These gases trap heat, which makes the planet warm even faster. Scientists monitor permafrost and measure how much carbon it's releasing as it thaws, giving them clues about how much greenhouse gas might be released in the future. This research is crucial for predicting the pace of climate change and understanding how to slow it down.

Arctic research is also valuable because it helps scientists understand the past. Ice cores from glaciers contain tiny bubbles of air that were trapped long ago, preserving samples of ancient atmospheres. By studying the gases in these bubbles, scientists can learn what Earth's climate was like thousands of years ago. They can see how levels of carbon dioxide and other greenhouse gases have changed over time and how Earth's temperature responded. This information helps scientists see patterns in climate history and predict how our current actions might affect the climate in the future. These ice cores act like history books, teaching us about past climate changes and helping us prepare for what lies ahead.

Arctic animals also tell us a lot about Earth's environment. Polar bears, walruses, caribou, and migratory birds are all facing new challenges as their habitats change. These animals are like "indicator species," which means that changes in their behavior or population can reveal information about the health of the ecosystem. For instance, polar bears' hunting patterns change as sea ice melts, and this impacts other animals in the food chain. By observing these animals, scientists can gather clues about the broader ecosystem and the effects of climate change. Arctic wildlife studies are essential for understanding the health of polar ecosystems and the challenges that animals – and humans – may face as conditions continue to change.

The Arctic's icy environment also holds clues about the ocean's chemistry. As sea ice forms, it releases salt into the surrounding water, creating dense, salty currents that sink and flow toward the equator. These currents play a role in the ocean's chemical balance, including the amount of carbon it can store. The ocean acts as a "carbon sink," absorbing carbon dioxide from the atmosphere. But as the Arctic changes, this balance could be disrupted, affecting how much carbon the ocean can hold. By studying these interactions, scientists are learning more about how the ocean helps regulate the amount of carbon dioxide in the atmosphere and slows down global warming.

One area of Arctic research that has captured attention is the study of microbes living in the ice and permafrost. These tiny organisms are adapted to survive in extreme conditions, and they may hold secrets to understanding life in other harsh environments, like Mars. Microbes are an important part of the ecosystem, breaking down organic matter and releasing nutrients back into the environment. But as permafrost thaws, these microbes begin to decompose long-frozen plant material, which releases carbon dioxide and methane. Studying these microbes helps scientists understand the role they play in the carbon cycle and how they might impact future greenhouse gas levels.

Through all this research, scientists are building a more complete picture of how Earth's systems work together. The Arctic might seem like a distant, frozen world, but it's connected to life everywhere – in big ways and small. Each discovery in the Arctic adds another piece to the puzzle of understanding our planet's climate, ecosystems, and even the origins of life. This knowledge doesn't just stay in scientific journals; it shapes policies, informs conservation efforts, and inspires people around the world to protect our planet.

7

SURVIVING IN THE ARCTIC

One of the first challenges that Arctic explorers and scientists face is the intense cold. Even taking a breath in the Arctic can feel different, as the air is so cold it almost stings your lungs. To protect against these freezing temperatures, Arctic adventurers wear layers of insulated clothing. They start with a base layer made from materials like wool or synthetic fabrics that trap body heat but let moisture escape. On top of that, they add a thicker layer for warmth, followed by an outer layer that blocks the wind and keeps snow and ice from getting in. The goal is to stay warm and dry without getting too sweaty because sweat can freeze and make you even colder.

Every part of the body needs protection, especially the hands, feet, and face. Frostbite, which happens when skin and tissue freeze, is a real danger. To avoid it, Arctic travelers wear thick mittens and gloves, insulated boots, and balaclavas or face masks that cover everything except their eyes. Sometimes, they even wear goggles to keep their eyes from freezing in the bitter cold. These clothes are often bulky and can make movement challenging, but staying warm and avoiding frostbite is the top priority.

Moving across the snow and ice is another challenge. In the Arctic, deep snow and icy surfaces can make walking difficult, especially when carrying heavy equipment. Explorers use special tools to help them get around, like snowshoes or skis. Snowshoes spread out a person's weight, making it easier to walk on top of deep snow without sinking. Skis can also be helpful, allowing scientists to glide across the snow and move faster than they would on foot. Some researchers even use sleds or dog teams to carry their equipment, which helps them cover longer distances without getting exhausted.

In recent years, snowmobiles have become a popular way to travel across the Arctic, but they come with risks. Snowmobiles are fast and powerful, making it easier to cover large distances, but they also require fuel, which is heavy to carry and not always available. Additionally, if a snowmobile breaks down in the middle of nowhere, it can be dangerous. For this reason, many Arctic travelers carry spare parts, tools, and emergency supplies to fix their snowmobiles if something goes wrong.

Navigating in the Arctic can be tricky. There are no roads, and the landscape is often featureless, with endless stretches of snow and ice. It's easy to get lost, especially in bad weather when visibility is low. To help them find their way, scientists use GPS devices and compasses. However, technology isn't foolproof, especially in extreme cold, where batteries can die quickly. Many explorers learn to navigate by looking at landmarks, like distant mountains or the sun, and they keep track of their direction carefully. Experienced Arctic travelers often carry paper maps as a backup in case their technology fails.

Safety in the Arctic also depends on understanding the environment, including the behavior of the ice. Sea ice, which forms on the surface of the ocean, can be thick and strong in some places but thin and dangerous in others. It's constantly shifting and breaking up, creating cracks and leads – open areas of water surrounded by ice. These leads can be hidden under snow or look solid from a distance, which makes them especially risky. Scientists and explorers learn to test the ice with poles, check for changes in color or texture, and stay alert for signs of cracking sounds, which can signal that the ice is weakening.

Arctic scientists also face the challenge of living in remote research stations for weeks or even months at a time. These stations are often located in isolated places, far from towns or rescue services. Each station is stocked with food, water, and medical supplies, and everyone working there learns basic first aid and survival skills. Some stations have communication systems to stay in contact with the outside world, but bad weather can interfere with radio signals or satellite phones. To prepare for emergencies, research teams create detailed plans for what to do if someone gets injured or if they need to be evacuated.

Meals at Arctic research stations are also carefully planned. Fresh food is hard to come by, especially in winter, so many stations rely on canned, dried, or frozen food that can last for months. Explorers and scientists burn a lot of energy just staying warm, so their meals are high in calories to help them stay energized. Hot drinks, like tea or coffee, are also popular because they help keep everyone warm. Some stations grow small amounts of fresh food, like herbs or sprouts, in greenhouses or hydroponic gardens, adding a welcome boost of nutrients to their diet.

Sleep in the Arctic can be unusual, especially in the summer or winter when there is constant daylight or darkness. During the long Arctic winter, darkness lasts 24 hours a day, which can be hard on the body and mind. Scientists use special lamps to mimic sunlight, which helps them maintain a regular sleep schedule and feel more energized. In summer, blackout curtains help block out the constant daylight, making it easier to sleep. Scientists learn to adjust their routines, relying on clocks and routines to keep their days organized, even when the sun is shining at midnight or completely absent.

Arctic explorers and scientists also need to be prepared for encounters with wildlife. The Arctic is home to polar bears, which are powerful predators and skilled hunters. Polar bears usually avoid humans, but in some areas, scientists may come across one while working. To stay safe, researchers learn to recognize bear tracks and signs, like claw marks or droppings. Many Arctic research teams carry bear spray or flares to scare off a curious bear, and they store food securely to avoid attracting animals to their camps. Some stations have fences or alarms to alert them if a bear gets too close.

Another danger is the Arctic's unpredictable weather. Blizzards can strike suddenly, bringing fierce winds and whiteout conditions where it's impossible to see even a few feet ahead. Temperatures can drop in minutes, and frostbite or hypothermia can become a risk. When a storm hits, scientists often "hunker down," staying indoors or finding shelter until the storm passes. Research stations and camps are designed to withstand strong winds, and they're stocked with enough supplies to keep everyone safe and comfortable if they're stuck indoors for days. Teams also carry emergency shelters and survival kits, which can include blankets, food, and water, in case they're caught out in a storm.

Essential Arctic Gear

Venturing into the Arctic means facing a world of ice, snow, and extreme cold. To survive here, explorers and scientists need special gear that keeps them warm, safe, and ready for anything the Arctic throws their way. From super-insulated parkas to tough, weather-proof tents, each piece of equipment is carefully chosen and tested for the harsh conditions. Let's explore the essential gear that Arctic adventurers rely on, from the clothes they wear to the shelters they sleep in, each designed to help them thrive in one of the coldest places on Earth.

At the top of the list is the parka, a thick, heavy coat that covers from head to knee, offering ultimate protection from the freezing temperatures and cutting winds. Parkas are designed to trap body heat, keeping the cold out and warmth in, even when it's bitterly cold. They're often filled with down feathers or synthetic insulation, which creates air pockets that trap heat. The outside of the parka is made from a waterproof and windproof material, helping block out snow and icy winds. Many parkas have fur-lined hoods, which serve more than just fashion – the fur helps break up the wind around the face, creating a small "warm bubble" that makes breathing more comfortable in the biting cold.

Under the parka, layers are the secret to staying warm. Arctic explorers dress in three main layers: the base layer, the mid-layer, and the outer layer. The base layer is closest to the skin, and it's made of materials like merino wool or synthetic fibers that wick moisture away. This is important because sweat can freeze in the Arctic, making a person feel even colder. The mid-layer is usually a fleece or down jacket that provides insulation, keeping warmth close to the body. Then, the parka goes on top, acting as a shield against the wind and snow. This layering system allows scientists to adjust their clothing, adding or removing layers depending on how cold or active they are.

Keeping hands and feet warm is just as important. Frostbite can set in quickly in the Arctic, especially on fingers, toes, and other exposed areas. For hands, most people wear two layers of gloves: a thin, lightweight glove that allows for movement and a heavier mitten that goes over the top. Mittens are warmer than gloves because fingers stay together, creating more warmth. Arctic mittens are often insulated with down or synthetic materials, and some have extra-long cuffs that go over jacket sleeves to keep out snow and cold air.

Feet are protected by special Arctic boots, which are designed to keep feet warm and dry in deep snow and freezing temperatures. These boots are typically made from thick, waterproof materials and have insulation that surrounds the entire foot. Many Arctic boots have removable liners, which can be taken out and dried overnight to keep feet dry. The soles are often made with materials that grip icy surfaces, helping explorers keep their footing on slippery terrain. Socks play an important role too – most people wear wool or thermal socks that keep feet warm without making them sweaty.

Headgear is essential, as most body heat is lost through the head. Explorers wear hats, face masks, and sometimes balaclavas that cover the head, neck, and face. These are usually made from wool or fleece, providing warmth and breathability. A good Arctic hat will cover the ears and have a snug fit to prevent any wind from sneaking in. For extra warmth, many Arctic explorers pull up the hood of their parka, which adds another layer of protection against the cold and wind. Goggles are often worn as well, especially in windy conditions, to protect the eyes from frostbite and blowing snow.

When it's time to set up camp, Arctic explorers rely on special tents designed to withstand extreme cold, high winds, and heavy snowfall. Arctic tents are made from tough, weather-resistant materials that can handle the elements. They're often shaped like domes or tunnels, which helps them stay stable in strong winds and prevents snow from piling up on top. The poles are flexible and strong, made to bend in the wind without breaking. Inside, Arctic tents have a double-wall design, with an inner layer that keeps warmth in and an outer layer that blocks the wind and snow.

Setting up a tent in the Arctic can be challenging, especially in icy conditions. To secure the tent, explorers use snow stakes, which are different from regular tent pegs. Snow stakes are wide and designed to be buried in the snow, providing a solid anchor that keeps the tent in place, even in blustery weather. Once the tent is set up, explorers dig a small trench around it to keep snow from blowing inside. In really cold weather, they might pile snow around the base of the tent to add insulation, keeping it warmer inside.

Inside the tent, sleeping bags are a critical part of staying warm. Arctic sleeping bags are thick, insulated, and specially designed to trap body heat. They're often mummy-shaped, which means they're narrower at the feet and wider at the shoulders, helping reduce heat loss. Many Arctic sleeping bags are rated for temperatures as low as -40°F, which means they're incredibly warm. Some sleeping bags even have built-in hoods that wrap around the head, keeping explorers cozy from head to toe. For extra warmth, people might also use sleeping bag liners, which add another layer of insulation.

Sleeping pads are also essential in the Arctic. A sleeping pad goes underneath the sleeping bag, acting as a barrier between the person and the cold ground. Arctic sleeping pads are often inflatable or made from thick foam, creating a layer of air that keeps the cold from seeping through. Without a good sleeping pad, even the warmest sleeping bag wouldn't be enough to keep someone comfortable, as the cold ground would pull away their body heat.

For meals, Arctic explorers use compact stoves that work well in freezing temperatures. These stoves are designed to melt snow into water and heat up food, and they're usually powered by fuel that works reliably in the cold. Arctic stoves are often lightweight and portable, making them easy to carry from one campsite to another. Since fresh food is hard to keep in the Arctic, most explorers bring freeze-dried meals that can be rehydrated with hot water, providing a warm, nutritious meal after a long day in the cold. Drinking enough water is also essential, as dehydration can make it harder to stay warm.

Lighting is another key part of Arctic gear. During the long Arctic winter, it's dark almost all day, and even in summer, the weather can bring cloudy, dim conditions. Headlamps, flashlights, and lanterns are necessary for getting around safely and working in low light. Headlamps are especially useful because they leave hands free, allowing scientists and explorers to work, set up camp, or cook without needing to hold a light.

Lastly, everyone in the Arctic carries an emergency kit. These kits contain items like first aid supplies, extra food, fire-starting materials, and a small emergency shelter in case something goes wrong. Satellite phones or personal locator beacons are also part of the gear, allowing explorers to call for help if they're in trouble or need to be rescued. These communication tools are critical, especially in remote areas where regular cell phones don't work.

Basic Survival Tips for Extreme Environments

Surviving in the Arctic is all about being prepared, alert, and staying calm. Extreme environments like the Arctic are breathtaking and full of beauty, but they also come with risks that demand respect and caution. Scientists, explorers, and even tourists who venture into these frozen lands know they need to follow certain rules and survival strategies to stay safe. These aren't just random tips – they're time-tested practices that can make all the difference in a place where temperatures can plummet, the sun can disappear for months, and the landscape itself can seem as wild as any storm. Let's dive into some essential survival tips for handling the Arctic's extreme conditions.

One of the most important things to remember in the Arctic is to dress properly and in layers. The Arctic cold can be intense, with the temperature dropping far below freezing and the wind making it feel even colder. The key to staying warm is to dress in layers that trap heat but allow sweat to escape. A good starting layer is the base layer, made from wool or synthetic materials, which wicks moisture away from the body. Over that comes an insulating layer, such as fleece or down, which traps body heat. Finally, an outer layer, usually a windproof and waterproof jacket, protects against wind and snow. Each layer has a purpose, and together they create a warm, flexible shield against the cold.

Next, it's crucial to keep extremities – fingers, toes, and face – protected from frostbite. The Arctic cold can numb your skin in minutes, and if skin stays exposed too long, frostbite can occur. Wearing thick gloves or mittens, warm socks, and insulated boots helps keep these vulnerable parts safe. Mittens are usually warmer than gloves because fingers stay close together, sharing warmth. For the face, many

Arctic travelers use balaclavas or masks that cover their nose and mouth, and sometimes even their eyes. A hood pulled over the head, along with a warm hat, completes the setup, creating a warm pocket around the face.

Staying dry is another essential survival tip. Getting wet in the Arctic, whether from sweat, snow, or melting ice, can lead to dangerous situations, as wet clothes lose their ability to insulate. To avoid this, it's important to avoid overheating. If you're moving around a lot, like hiking or setting up camp, you might need to remove a layer to keep from sweating too much. Arctic explorers often use "breathable" materials that let moisture escape but keep the cold air out. If clothes do get wet, finding a way to dry them out – either by hanging them up inside a tent or wearing them close to the body to warm them up – is essential for staying warm.

In the Arctic, hydration is as important as staying warm. It might seem strange to think about drinking water in such a cold environment, but the dry air and the physical effort needed to move around in the cold can quickly lead to dehydration. Many Arctic travelers carry insulated water bottles or thermoses to keep water from freezing. They also melt snow for water, but it's essential to remember that snow alone doesn't provide enough water for hydration; it has to be melted first. Drinking warm liquids like tea or soup not only keeps the body hydrated but also provides warmth, making it a great survival habit.

Knowing how to build a shelter is another fundamental Arctic survival skill. If you're out in the open and a storm hits, a sturdy shelter can mean the difference between comfort and danger. For temporary shelter, snow can actually be a great material. Snow is an excellent insulator because it traps air, which can help keep the inside of a shelter warmer than the outside air. People have used snow to create igloos, snow caves, and other types of shelter for centuries. To build a snow cave, find a deep snowdrift, dig an entrance tunnel, and then hollow out a small room inside. It's important to create a small ventilation hole to allow fresh air in. Once inside, body heat will start to warm the space, making it much more comfortable than the open air.

Food is also critical in the Arctic, where the cold can burn calories faster than normal. Arctic travelers need to eat high-calorie foods to stay energized and warm. This might include dried meats, nuts, chocolate, or other high-energy foods that are easy to carry and don't freeze solid. Eating regularly keeps up energy levels and generates heat, helping to ward off the cold. Many people snack throughout the day instead of relying on large meals, which helps keep their energy levels steady. In addition to calories, warm food and drinks add to the feeling of warmth, making mealtime a good morale booster as well as a necessity.

Paying attention to the weather is another crucial survival strategy in the Arctic. Arctic weather can change quickly, going from calm to stormy in a matter of minutes. Strong winds, snowstorms, and blizzards can make it impossible to see, move, or even stay warm. Before setting out for any activity, checking the weather forecast and watching for changes in the sky can help you avoid getting caught in a dangerous situation. During a storm, it's safest to find shelter and wait it out. Arctic explorers and scientists often carry extra supplies, like food, water, and emergency blankets, to help them stay safe if they need to take shelter for a while.

In remote Arctic areas, navigation can be a real challenge. The landscape can look similar for miles, with snow-covered fields and frozen lakes stretching in every direction. This can make it hard to know which way to go. GPS devices are helpful, but the cold can drain batteries quickly, so it's essential to bring extra power sources or rely on old-fashioned tools like maps and compasses as a backup. Learning to recognize natural landmarks, like mountain ranges or rivers, can also help explorers find their way. In the Arctic, getting lost isn't just inconvenient; it can be dangerous, which makes careful navigation a top priority.

Awareness of wildlife is another survival tip to remember. Polar bears, for example, roam parts of the Arctic, and while they usually avoid humans, they are curious animals and skilled hunters. If traveling in areas where polar bears are known to live, Arctic travelers carry bear spray or flares to scare off any animals that come too close. They also store food securely, keeping it away from sleeping areas to avoid attracting animals. Making noise while moving through the landscape can also alert animals to your presence, reducing the chances of a surprise encounter.

Finally, staying calm is one of the most valuable survival skills in any extreme environment. In the Arctic, challenges can arise quickly, from sudden weather changes to unexpected gear problems. In these situations, panicking can make things worse, leading to poor decisions or wasted energy. By staying calm and focused, explorers can think clearly, assess their situation, and take steps to stay safe. Arctic explorers train themselves to respond thoughtfully, understanding that careful planning and a clear head can get them through most challenges they face.

8

PROTECTING THE ARCTIC

The Arctic is like a giant freezer at the top of the world, holding secrets of Earth's history and playing a huge role in keeping our planet's climate balanced. Its icy landscapes, incredible wildlife, and unique ecosystems make it a place of wonder and mystery. But the Arctic is changing faster than ever before, and these changes are affecting not just the animals and people who live there, but everyone on Earth. This is why protecting the Arctic has become a priority for scientists, conservationists, and even governments around the world. Arctic conservation isn't just about saving polar bears or preserving glaciers; it's about protecting a part of our planet that helps keep everything in balance.

One of the most important reasons to protect the Arctic is because of its role in regulating the Earth's climate. The Arctic acts like a giant reflector, bouncing sunlight back into space. When sunlight hits the bright, white ice, much of it reflects away, helping to keep the Arctic (and the rest of the world) cool. But as temperatures rise, more ice melts, revealing darker surfaces like the ocean. Unlike ice, the dark ocean absorbs more heat, which speeds up warming. This is known as the albedo effect, and it's one reason why the Arctic is warming faster than other places on Earth. By protecting the Arctic, we're also helping to keep the planet from warming up too quickly.

Another reason conservation is so critical in the Arctic is because of the animals that call it home. From polar bears to walruses, and from Arctic foxes to snowy owls, the Arctic is a place of unique wildlife, each species adapted perfectly to its harsh environment. Polar bears, for example, depend on sea ice to hunt for seals, their main food source. As the ice melts, they lose their hunting grounds, forcing them to travel longer distances and use more energy to find food. Many polar bears are becoming thinner and weaker, and some are even at risk of starvation. Walruses, too, need sea ice for resting between dives, and with less ice, they're gathering in large groups on land, where food is scarcer, and there's more risk of injury.

The Arctic's marine life is also under pressure. Fish populations, like Arctic char and cod, are changing as ocean temperatures rise, and plankton blooms are shifting. Plankton may be tiny, but they form the base of the Arctic food web, feeding fish, which in turn feed larger animals like seals, whales, and seabirds. A change in the timing or location of plankton blooms can affect the entire food chain. Arctic conservation helps protect this delicate balance, ensuring that each link in the chain remains strong, from the smallest plankton to the largest polar bears.

Indigenous communities in the Arctic have lived in harmony with their environment for thousands of years, relying on traditional knowledge and practices to survive and thrive. These communities have a deep connection to the land, animals, and seasons, and they know the Arctic better than anyone else. Climate change and other threats to the Arctic are not just environmental issues for them; they're also cultural ones. As ice melts and animal populations shift, Indigenous communities face challenges in hunting, fishing, and preserving their way of life.

Conservation efforts often work with these communities, respecting and including their knowledge and voices in decision-making, because they are vital to understanding and protecting the Arctic.

One of the greatest threats to the Arctic is pollution, especially plastic and chemicals that drift into the region from other parts of the world. Currents carry plastic debris and toxic chemicals from thousands of miles away, where they accumulate in the Arctic's cold waters. This pollution harms marine life, as animals like seals, fish, and seabirds can mistake plastic for food. Toxic chemicals build up in the food chain, affecting not only animals but also the people who rely on them for food. Protecting the Arctic means addressing pollution, reducing plastic waste, and finding ways to stop harmful chemicals from reaching this sensitive environment.

Another concern is oil drilling and resource extraction. The Arctic holds vast reserves of oil and natural gas, and some companies want to extract these resources. But drilling in the Arctic is risky, and an oil spill in these icy waters would be devastating. Cold temperatures and remote locations make it extremely difficult to clean up oil spills, and the impact on the environment would last for years, if not decades. In addition to the immediate danger, drilling for oil and gas releases more carbon dioxide into the atmosphere, contributing to climate change and melting ice. Conservationists are working to protect areas of the Arctic from drilling, promoting clean energy alternatives to reduce the need for fossil fuels.

Protecting the Arctic isn't just about what happens there; it's about how it affects the entire planet. As the Arctic warms, permafrost – the permanently frozen ground – is starting to thaw. Permafrost holds huge amounts of carbon, and as it thaws, it releases carbon dioxide and methane into the atmosphere. These greenhouse gases contribute to global warming, creating a feedback loop that makes the Arctic warm even faster. By conserving the Arctic, we can help slow down the release of these gases and reduce the pace of climate change.

Conservation efforts in the Arctic include creating protected areas, limiting resource extraction, and conducting research to monitor changes. Protected areas are zones where human activity is limited or banned, giving wildlife a safe place to live and thrive. These areas can be as small as a single island or as large as an entire bay. Scientists often conduct research in protected areas to understand more about the Arctic ecosystem and to see how changes are affecting plants and animals. Monitoring helps conservationists make informed decisions, guiding efforts to protect the Arctic's most vulnerable habitats.

International cooperation is also key to Arctic conservation. The Arctic is surrounded by countries like Canada, Russia, Norway, and the United States, and each of these countries has a stake in the region. Conservation efforts often involve agreements between these countries, setting rules for shipping, fishing, and resource extraction. One such agreement is the Arctic Council, a group of Arctic nations and Indigenous organizations that work together to promote sustainable development and environmental protection in the Arctic. By working together, these countries can address issues that no single nation could tackle alone, such as pollution and climate change.

One of the most inspiring aspects of Arctic conservation is how many people from different backgrounds are coming together to protect this unique region. Scientists, Indigenous leaders, conservationists, and even kids are finding ways to raise awareness and make a difference. Schools around the world are learning about the Arctic, and students are taking action by organizing clean-up projects, reducing plastic use, and speaking up about climate change. Artists and filmmakers are capturing the beauty of the Arctic, bringing its landscapes and wildlife to people who may never see it in person. This global effort shows that while the Arctic may be far away, it's connected to us all.

Threats to the Arctic

Climate change is probably the most well-known threat facing the Arctic today. Temperatures in the Arctic are rising faster than anywhere else on the planet, and this warming is causing major changes. One of the most noticeable effects of climate change in the Arctic is the loss of sea ice. Sea ice forms when the ocean's surface freezes, creating a thick, icy layer that stretches across the Arctic Ocean. This ice grows in winter and shrinks in summer, but for thousands of years, enough ice has survived each summer to create a stable habitat. Now, however, the ice is melting more rapidly each year, and scientists predict that we could see ice-free Arctic summers within our lifetimes.

This loss of sea ice is more than just a visual change; it affects everything from the animals that rely on ice to the entire global climate system. Polar bears, for instance, use sea ice as their hunting grounds. They roam across the ice, looking for seals, which are their primary food source. Without enough ice, polar bears have to swim longer distances or move onto land, where food is much scarcer. This puts them at risk of starvation and disrupts their way of life. Walruses, too, rely on sea ice for resting between dives, and without it, they're forced to gather on land in large groups, which can lead to overcrowding and increased competition for food.

The shrinking ice also impacts the ocean. Sea ice reflects sunlight, helping keep the Arctic cool. When the ice melts, it exposes the dark ocean water beneath, which absorbs more heat from the sun. This warming of the ocean can change currents, disrupt marine life, and even influence weather patterns far from the Arctic. The loss of ice is like taking away a layer of protection, making the Arctic even more vulnerable to warming. This process is called the albedo effect, and it's one of the reasons why the Arctic is warming faster than other regions.

Glaciers and permafrost in the Arctic are also being affected by climate change. Glaciers are massive rivers of ice that slowly flow down from mountains, and they hold huge amounts of frozen water. As the Arctic warms, glaciers are melting more quickly, adding freshwater to the ocean and contributing to rising sea levels. Rising sea levels are a concern for people around the world, especially those who live in coastal cities and islands. The melting of Arctic glaciers is just one part of the global puzzle of rising seas, but it's an important one.

Permafrost, or permanently frozen ground, is another critical part of the Arctic that's being changed by warming temperatures. Permafrost holds huge amounts of carbon, stored in frozen plants and soil. When permafrost thaws, this carbon is released as greenhouse gases like carbon dioxide and methane, which trap heat in the atmosphere and speed up climate change. This creates a feedback loop, where warming causes permafrost to thaw, which releases more greenhouse gases, which then cause more warming. Scientists are worried that if too much permafrost thaws, it could add a lot more carbon to the atmosphere, making climate change even harder to slow down.

Pollution is another major threat to the Arctic, and it comes in many forms. Even though the Arctic is far from most industrial areas, pollution from other parts of the world makes its way there through air and ocean currents. One of the biggest problems is plastic pollution. Tiny pieces of plastic, called microplastics, are found throughout the Arctic's ice, snow, and water. These plastics can come from everyday items like plastic bags, bottles, and packaging, which break down into smaller and smaller pieces but never fully disappear.

Microplastics are a danger to marine life, as fish, birds, and other animals may mistake them for food. When animals eat plastic, it can harm their digestive systems and even lead to death. These plastics don't just affect the animals that eat them directly; they move up the food chain, affecting larger animals and even people who eat Arctic fish and seafood. Researchers are finding plastic in areas once thought to be untouched by pollution, showing just how far-reaching this problem has become.

Chemicals are another type of pollution affecting the Arctic. Toxic chemicals like mercury, pesticides, and industrial pollutants travel long distances in the air and water, eventually settling in the Arctic. These chemicals can build up in the bodies of animals, especially those at the top of the food chain, like polar bears, seals, and even Indigenous people who rely on traditional hunting and fishing for food. This process, called bioaccumulation, means that animals absorb these chemicals over time, and as larger animals eat smaller ones, the concentration of toxins increases. This can cause health problems, including reproductive issues and weakened immune systems, making it harder for animals to survive in an already challenging environment.

Oil spills and industrial activities also pose a risk to the Arctic. As ice melts, some companies are interested in drilling for oil and natural gas in the Arctic Ocean. Drilling in these icy waters is risky, and an oil spill would be incredibly difficult to clean up. Cold temperatures slow down the natural breakdown of oil, meaning that any spill could linger for years, harming marine life and polluting the water and coastline. Oil spills can be deadly for animals, coating their fur or feathers, making it hard for them to stay warm and clean, and affecting the food sources they depend on. The Arctic's remote location makes it hard to respond quickly to spills, which only increases the damage.

Noise pollution is another issue that affects the Arctic, though it might not be as visible as plastic or chemicals. As more ships travel through the Arctic due to melting ice, the noise from engines can disrupt marine animals, particularly whales and seals that rely on sound to communicate, navigate, and find food. The Arctic is typically a very quiet place, and these animals have evolved to live in a world of natural sounds. Increased noise can cause stress and interfere with their natural behaviors, putting additional pressure on species that are already struggling with habitat loss.

What Kids Can Do to Help Protect the Arctic

The Arctic might feel far away, but everyone can play a part in helping to protect it, including kids. Even though you may not live near icy oceans or see polar bears in your backyard, the choices you make every day can help keep the Arctic safe and healthy. When you learn about the Arctic and the challenges it faces, you're already taking the first step. Every small action, whether at home, in school, or in your community, can add up to make a big difference. Let's explore some simple but powerful ways kids can help protect this amazing region and all the animals and people who depend on it.

One of the easiest ways to help protect the Arctic is by using less plastic. Plastic waste is one of the biggest pollution problems in the world, and a lot of it ends up in the ocean, eventually reaching even the most remote places like the Arctic. Every piece of plastic that ends up in the ocean can harm animals, including Arctic seabirds, seals, and fish, who can mistake plastic for food. By using less plastic, you can help reduce the amount of waste that might end up far away in the Arctic.

You can start by saying "no" to single-use plastics, like plastic straws, bags, and bottles. Instead, try using reusable items, like a metal straw, a reusable water bottle, or a cloth bag. Bringing your own lunch in a reusable container instead of a plastic bag is another great way to help. Every piece of plastic you avoid using is one less piece that could end up harming wildlife. If you see litter around your neighborhood, picking it up and throwing it away properly keeps it from blowing into rivers or oceans, where it could eventually travel to faraway places.

Another powerful way to help the Arctic is by learning about energy and how it affects our planet. Burning fossil fuels, like coal, oil, and natural gas, creates carbon dioxide, a greenhouse gas that traps heat in the atmosphere and contributes to climate change. This is one reason the Arctic is warming so quickly. Even though kids don't drive cars or use a lot of electricity, there are still things you can do to help reduce energy use and lower the amount of carbon dioxide going into the atmosphere.

Turning off lights when you leave a room, unplugging electronics when you're not using them, and taking shorter showers are all easy ways to save energy. You can also remind your family to do these things, turning it into a fun challenge to see how much energy you can save together. Learning about renewable energy, like solar and wind power, is another way to become an Arctic protector. Renewable energy sources don't produce greenhouse gases, which makes them better for the planet. When you understand the importance of using clean energy, you can even inspire others to make choices that help the environment.

Supporting conservation projects is another way to help the Arctic, and you can do it from right where you are. Many conservation groups are working to protect Arctic animals, clean up pollution, and monitor changes in the Arctic ecosystem. You can help by learning about these organizations and, if possible, supporting them. Some conservation groups offer kid-friendly programs that allow you to symbolically "adopt" an Arctic animal, like a polar bear or Arctic fox. These programs usually involve a small donation, and in return, you might receive an adoption certificate, a photo of your chosen animal, and updates on how the organization is helping protect its habitat.

If you're interested in getting involved, talk to your parents, teachers, or friends about starting a fundraising project for an Arctic conservation organization. You could organize a bake sale, set up a lemonade stand, or create handmade crafts to sell, with the proceeds going to protect the Arctic. Even a small donation can help fund important projects, like rescuing injured animals, researching climate change, or cleaning up plastic from the Arctic Ocean.

Reducing waste is another simple way to protect the Arctic, and it's something you can do every day. Besides cutting down on plastic, try to reduce how much you throw away overall. Recycle whenever you can, and compost food scraps if it's possible in your area. The less waste we produce, the less energy is needed to dispose of it, which reduces greenhouse gases and helps the Arctic.

You can also think about how to reuse items instead of throwing them away. For example, you could turn empty jars into containers for art supplies, or old T-shirts into cleaning rags. Reusing items keeps them out of landfills, where they would release gases that contribute to climate change. You might even consider organizing a "zero waste" week with your family or friends, challenging each other to throw away as little as possible. Not only does this help the environment, but it's also a fun way to get creative with reusing and recycling.

Learning and sharing what you know about the Arctic is one of the most important things you can do. When you understand why the Arctic is special and why it needs protection, you can inspire others to care too. Talk to your friends, family, and classmates about what you've learned. You could create a presentation for school, write a story or poem about the Arctic, or even make a poster that shows the importance of protecting the Arctic. Spreading awareness helps more people understand how they can make a difference, and it creates a chain reaction that reaches further than you might think.

If you enjoy art, you can use your creativity to bring attention to the Arctic. Draw pictures of Arctic animals, make a collage of Arctic landscapes, or create a video about climate change. You could share your artwork on social media (with permission from an adult) or organize an Arctic awareness day at school. By using art to tell a story, you help people connect emotionally with the Arctic, making them more likely to want to protect it.

9

FUN FACTS ABOUT THE ARCTIC

One of the most famous Arctic weather phenomena is the aurora, often called the northern lights. Imagine looking up at the night sky and seeing it filled with colorful, swirling lights that move and dance as if they have a mind of their own. These lights can be green, pink, red, purple, or even blue, and they often stretch across the sky like giant ribbons or waves. The aurora is caused by particles from the sun interacting with Earth's magnetic field. When these particles hit the atmosphere, they create bursts of light that appear to dance in the sky.

The best places to see the aurora are in the far north, including places like Norway, Alaska, and Canada, where the nights are long and dark in the winter. Sometimes, the lights are so bright that you can even see them reflected on the snow-covered ground below. Seeing an aurora is something people travel from all over the world to experience, and for those lucky enough to witness it, it's a sight they'll never forget. In fact, many Arctic communities have special festivals during winter to celebrate this incredible light show.

Another unique Arctic weather phenomenon is the snowstorm, or blizzard, which can transform the landscape in a matter of hours. Snowstorms in the Arctic aren't just about snow falling gently from the sky – they're often intense, with powerful winds that make it nearly impossible to see even a few feet in front of you. These storms can last for hours, sometimes even days, piling up snow that covers everything in sight. The wind in an Arctic snowstorm can blow the snow around so much that it feels like it's coming from every direction. This is called a "whiteout," and it makes the world around you look like a blank sheet of paper. In a whiteout, it's easy to lose your sense of direction, which is why people in the Arctic have learned to be careful and wait out these storms indoors if they can.

Snow itself is interesting in the Arctic. Most people think of snow as just frozen water, but Arctic snow comes in many different forms. You can have fluffy snow that's light and soft, or heavy snow that packs tightly together. Snowflakes form when water vapor freezes around tiny particles in the air, and they can have hundreds of different shapes, including simple six-sided crystals or more complex designs that look like tiny stars. The temperature and moisture in the air affect how snowflakes form, which is why you might see different kinds of snow depending on the weather. In the Arctic, the snow can be so cold and dry that it doesn't melt together as easily, making it crunch loudly underfoot when you walk on it.

Another fascinating thing about the Arctic is the polar night, which happens in winter when the sun doesn't rise above the horizon for days, weeks, or even months, depending on how far north you are. Imagine going to bed in darkness, waking up in darkness, and spending the whole day without a single ray of sunlight. The polar night is one of the reasons why winters in the Arctic feel so unique – and why the aurora is even more special, lighting up the long, dark nights with its colors. Even though it sounds intense, people in the Arctic have adapted to this rhythm. They use special lamps to make up for the lack of sunlight and celebrate the return of the sun when it finally rises again.

In contrast to the polar night, the Arctic experiences the midnight sun in the summer. During this time, the sun doesn't set, shining 24 hours a day for days, weeks, or even months! It's as if the entire region is in a constant state of daylight, no matter the time of day. This endless daylight can make it tricky to know when to go to sleep, and some Arctic animals and plants rely on this extra sunlight to grow and feed as much as possible before the winter returns. For people, blackout curtains and sleep masks become essential during the midnight sun to help keep a regular sleep schedule.

Frost is another weather feature you'll see all over the Arctic. Frost happens when water vapor in the air freezes on cold surfaces, like windows, tree branches, or even your coat! In the Arctic, frost can form beautiful, intricate patterns that look almost like lace. You might see frost on plants, covering them in a sparkling, icy layer. When frost forms on windows, it creates swirls and shapes that look like something out of a fairy tale. The air in the Arctic is often very dry, but even a small amount of moisture can create these amazing frost patterns. In some Arctic communities, people make a tradition of photographing or drawing the frost patterns they see in winter.

Ice fog is another rare Arctic weather event. This happens when the air is so cold that tiny droplets of water freeze into crystals while floating in the air, creating a fog that looks like glittering dust. Unlike regular fog, which is just tiny droplets of water, ice fog is made of frozen particles. When light shines through ice fog, it can create halos or rings of light that look magical. Sometimes, you might even see "sun dogs," which are bright spots that appear on either side of the sun, almost like a second or third sun shining in the sky. Sun dogs are caused by the way light refracts, or bends, through ice crystals in the air, creating an effect that seems straight out of a storybook.

Finally, there's something called "diamond dust," a type of Arctic snowfall made up of tiny ice crystals that sparkle in the sunlight. Diamond dust often occurs on clear, cold days when there's no wind, and it falls slowly through the air, twinkling like glitter. These crystals are so small and light that they float, creating a shimmering effect. Diamond dust can create halos, too, and it's considered one of the most beautiful winter sights. When it falls, it feels like the air itself is filled with sparkles, turning a simple walk outside into a magical experience.

Strange but True: Arctic Mysteries and Legends

One of the most intriguing legends of the Arctic is the story of the Aurora Borealis, or northern lights. For centuries, people have looked up at the sky in awe as the colorful lights danced across the horizon. These lights can be green, purple, pink, or blue, and they seem to move like ribbons or waves in the night sky. While today we know that the auroras are caused by particles from the sun interacting with Earth's atmosphere, ancient Arctic peoples had their own explanations. Some believed that the lights were the spirits of their ancestors, dancing joyfully across the sky. Others thought they were messages from the gods, meant to guide or protect them. In Norse mythology, the northern lights were seen as reflections from the armor of the Valkyries, warrior maidens who took brave soldiers to the afterlife.

For the Inuit people of Canada and Greenland, the northern lights were often seen as a good omen, but they also had a spooky side. Some Inuit believed the lights could reach down and snatch people up into the sky. They thought the lights were spirits playing a game, tossing a walrus skull back and forth like a ball, and anyone who whistled at the lights would be taken by them. To stay safe, people avoided making noise while watching the auroras, fearing they might attract the attention of the mysterious lights. Today, the northern lights remain one of the most popular reasons people travel to the Arctic, hoping to witness this breathtaking phenomenon.

Another Arctic mystery that has puzzled people for centuries is the story of the "Vanishing Village." In 1930, a fur trapper named Joe Labelle stumbled upon an Inuit village on the shores of Lake Anjikuni in Canada's Nunavut territory. When he entered the village, he was shocked to find it completely empty. The fires were still burning, food was left on the tables, and dogs were tied up outside – but there wasn't a single person to be found. It was as if the entire village had vanished without a trace. Labelle reported what he saw, and a search was conducted, but the villagers were never found. Some say the story of the Vanishing Village is an Arctic legend rather than a true event, but it continues to capture the imagination of people who wonder what might have happened to the missing villagers.

Legends of strange creatures also thrive in the Arctic. One such creature is known as the Qalupalik, a mythical being from Inuit folklore. The Qalupalik is described as a creature that lives under the ice in the Arctic waters, with long hair and green, slimy skin. According to legend, the Qalupalik wears an amauti, a traditional Inuit parka with a pouch for carrying children, and it uses this pouch to snatch children who wander too close to the shore. The Qalupalik is said to have a distinctive humming sound that warns children not to get too close. This legend was often used by parents to keep their children safe, as the icy waters of the Arctic can be very dangerous.

Then there's the story of Sedna, the Inuit goddess of the sea. Sedna is a central figure in Inuit mythology, and her story explains the creation of sea animals like seals, walruses, and whales. According to legend, Sedna was once a beautiful young woman who fell into the sea under mysterious circumstances. As she struggled in the water, her fingers were cut off, and each finger transformed into a different sea creature. From that point on, Sedna became the goddess of the sea, ruling over all marine animals. Inuit hunters would offer prayers to Sedna before hunting, asking for her blessing and hoping she would provide food for their families. Sedna's story is both beautiful and tragic, reminding people of the close connection between the Inuit and the sea.

The Arctic is also home to mysterious sounds, sometimes called the "Arctic hum" or "bloop." Some travelers and scientists have reported hearing strange noises that seem to come from nowhere, echoing across the ice and snow. These sounds have been described as low rumbles, humming, or even booming noises. In certain places, like the small town of Igloolik in Canada, people have reported hearing these strange sounds for years. While some scientists believe these noises could be caused by shifting ice or underwater seismic activity, others think the source of the sounds is still unknown. The idea of a mysterious Arctic hum has inspired many to wonder what other secrets the Arctic might be hiding beneath its frozen surface.

Even the skies above the Arctic hold mysterious tales. The "Arctic mirage," or Fata Morgana, is an optical illusion that makes objects on the horizon look distorted or stretched. In the cold Arctic air, layers of warm and cold air can bend light, creating mirages. A ship far off on the ocean might appear to float in the air, or a distant iceberg might look like a giant, towering castle. Sailors and explorers traveling through the Arctic have reported seeing strange shapes on the horizon, from ghostly ships to floating cities. This phenomenon is named after Morgan le Fay, a magical figure from Arthurian legend who was said to create illusions. Fata Morgana mirages are common in polar regions, adding a bit of mystery to the Arctic landscape.

One of the most curious Arctic legends is the mystery of the "Arctic aliens." Over the years, there have been reports from explorers and travelers of strange, unexplainable sightings in the Arctic sky, including flashing lights, unusual objects, and unexplained movements. Some believe these sightings could be evidence of UFOs or extraterrestrial visitors, while others suggest they may simply be rare atmospheric phenomena. In the 1940s and 1950s, during the Cold War, both the United States and Soviet Union conducted secret operations in the Arctic, which could have led to some of these mysterious sightings. Whatever the cause, the idea of "Arctic aliens" adds to the allure of this faraway land.

The vastness and isolation of the Arctic have also led to stories of lost explorers. One of the most famous tales is the Franklin Expedition, which set out in 1845 to find a Northwest Passage through the Arctic to connect the Atlantic and Pacific Oceans. Led by Sir John Franklin, the expedition included two ships, the HMS Erebus and HMS Terror, and over a hundred men. They vanished without a trace, leaving behind only a few clues, like letters, journals, and abandoned campsites. For years, people searched for the missing ships, and finally, in 2014, one of them was found beneath the icy waters near King William Island in Canada. The story of the Franklin Expedition remains one of the Arctic's greatest mysteries, sparking books, documentaries, and theories about what really happened to the crew.

Record-Breaking Facts about the Arctic

One of the first records that comes to mind is the cold. The Arctic is known for its freezing temperatures, but just how cold does it get? The coldest temperature ever recorded in the Arctic was -93°F (-69°C) in the town of Verkhoyansk, Russia, in 1892. Verkhoyansk is located within the Arctic Circle, where winter temperatures can drop to unbelievably low levels. But Verkhoyansk isn't alone in this record-breaking chill – Oymyakon, another Arctic town in Russia, also experienced -89°F (-67°C) in 1933, making it one of the coldest inhabited places on Earth. Imagine living in a place so cold that, in winter, your breath freezes instantly, creating a tiny cloud of ice crystals!

But while it holds records for cold, the Arctic can also get surprisingly warm during the summer. The warmest temperature ever recorded in the Arctic Circle was 100.4°F (38°C) in Verkhoyansk in June 2020. This might sound strange for the Arctic, but these extreme highs are happening more frequently due to climate change. During Arctic summers, temperatures above freezing aren't unusual, and places like Alaska and northern Canada can experience warm, sunny days where people can wear T-shirts! These temperatures remind us that the Arctic isn't always frozen and that summer brings a whole different feel to this region.

When it comes to animal migrations, the Arctic is home to some record-breakers. The Arctic tern, a small seabird, makes the longest migration of any animal on Earth. Every year, this bird flies from its breeding grounds in the Arctic all the way to Antarctica and back, covering a round trip of about 44,000 miles (70,800 kilometers)! This incredible journey allows the Arctic tern to experience two summers each year, one in the Arctic and one in Antarctica. Arctic terns live up to 30 years, meaning one bird might travel more than a million miles in its lifetime – that's like going to the moon and back twice!

Another impressive traveler in the Arctic is the caribou, also known as reindeer in Europe. Caribou undertake the longest migration of any land animal, covering up to 3,000 miles (4,800 kilometers) every year. These journeys are essential for finding food and safe places to give birth. Caribou are specially adapted for these long treks, with strong legs and wide hooves that help them move through deep snow and cross rivers. Their herds can include thousands of individuals, creating a spectacular sight as they travel across the Arctic tundra in search of food and shelter.

The Arctic Ocean is the smallest and shallowest of the world's oceans, but it holds some impressive records of its own. Did you know the Arctic Ocean contains more ice than any other ocean? Its sea ice is usually several feet thick, but in places, it can reach up to 15 feet (4.6 meters) thick. This ice forms a frozen cap over the ocean, creating a habitat for animals like polar bears, seals, and walruses. The ice also helps regulate Earth's temperature by reflecting sunlight, making the Arctic Ocean an important part of the global climate system.

Speaking of polar bears, these iconic Arctic

animals are also record holders. Polar bears are the largest land carnivores on Earth, with adult males weighing up to 1,500 pounds (680 kilograms) and standing around 10 feet (3 meters) tall on their hind legs. They have specially adapted bodies that allow them to survive in the extreme cold, including a layer of fat, thick fur, and even fur-covered feet to grip the ice. Polar bears are strong swimmers and can travel long distances in search of food. One polar bear was tracked swimming over 400 miles (640 kilometers) in one trip, showing just how tough and resilient these animals are.

The Arctic is also home to some of the longest-lasting days and nights on Earth. Near the North Pole, the sun rises and sets only once a year. This means that for six months, the Arctic experiences a period known as the "polar day," when the sun doesn't set at all, followed by a "polar night," when the sun doesn't rise. During the polar day, the sun stays above the horizon 24 hours a day, casting a golden glow that stretches across the landscape. When winter arrives, the polar night takes over, and the Arctic is plunged into darkness for months. This extreme cycle of light and dark is something only the Arctic and Antarctic experience, and it has a big impact on life in these regions.

Let's not forget about some of the Arctic's natural wonders, like the northern lights, or aurora borealis. The Arctic holds the record for some of the most spectacular aurora displays on Earth. These dancing lights are caused by charged particles from the sun interacting with Earth's magnetic field, creating waves of color across the night sky. Auroras can be seen in many parts of the world, but the Arctic is one of the best places to experience them. The lights can be seen in shades of green, pink, purple, and even red, and they often stretch across the sky in swirling ribbons or curtains. In the cold Arctic winter, these lights create a beautiful contrast against the dark, snowy landscape, adding to the magic of the region.

The Arctic is also home to some of the most ancient ice on Earth. Some glaciers in Greenland are over 100,000 years old, preserving layers of ice that hold clues about Earth's climate history. Scientists drill into these glaciers to collect ice cores, which are like time capsules of ancient air. By studying ice cores, scientists can learn about temperature changes, levels of greenhouse gases, and even volcanic eruptions from thousands of years ago. This ancient ice is a reminder of how long the Arctic has been frozen and the role it plays in Earth's history.

Another record-breaking feature of the Arctic is

its vast tundra. The Arctic tundra stretches across Alaska, Canada, Russia, and Greenland, creating one of the largest biomes in the world. Despite its cold temperatures and short growing season, the tundra is home to a surprising variety of plants and animals, including hardy mosses, lichens, wildflowers, and animals like Arctic foxes, hares, and snowy owls. The tundra is a crucial part of the Arctic ecosystem, and its plants help store carbon, which is important for regulating Earth's atmosphere.

Even in its remoteness, the Arctic holds records for adventure and exploration. In 1909, American explorer Robert Peary claimed to be the first person to reach the North Pole, although some historians debate whether he actually reached it. Since then, countless explorers have braved the cold to reach the "top of the world." The North Pole remains one of the most challenging places to visit, requiring special gear, courage, and endurance to navigate the frozen landscape. Today, a few adventurous travelers still attempt to reach the North Pole, keeping the spirit of Arctic exploration alive.

10

EXPLORING THE ARCTIC FROM HOME

Exploring the Arctic is something that many people dream about. It's a land of icy landscapes, polar bears, and swirling northern lights – a place that feels like it's on the edge of the world. But while it might be tricky to actually travel to the Arctic, especially for kids, there are still amazing ways to experience it right from home. Thanks to the internet and modern technology, we can explore the Arctic through virtual field trips, online videos, interactive maps, and even real-time animal cameras. These resources give us a way to "visit" the Arctic and learn about its unique environment, wildlife, and the people who live there without ever leaving home.

One of the most exciting ways to experience the

Arctic from home is through virtual field trips. A virtual field trip is just like a regular field trip, but instead of getting on a bus or plane, you "travel" through your computer screen. Many organizations and museums offer free virtual field trips to the Arctic, where you can explore icy landscapes, meet scientists, and see Arctic animals up close. Some of these field trips even include 360-degree videos, which allow you to "look around" as if you were standing right there in the Arctic.

For instance, Google Earth offers a virtual journey to the Arctic that includes stunning views of glaciers, icebergs, and snowy mountains. You can "fly over" the Arctic landscape, zoom in to see glaciers up close, and even learn about famous Arctic explorers. Another amazing virtual field trip is offered by the Ocean Exploration Trust, where you can explore the Arctic Ocean's deep-sea habitats and learn about the animals and ecosystems that thrive there. They provide videos and maps that take you beneath the icy waters, showing creatures like jellyfish, deep-sea fish, and even rare types of coral that live in the cold Arctic depths.

If you're curious about Arctic wildlife, live animal cameras are a fantastic way to get a close-up view of animals in their natural habitat. Many wildlife organizations set up cameras in the Arctic to observe animals like polar bears, seals, and snowy owls. These cameras stream live footage, which means you can watch what's happening in real time. For example, Explore.org has a live polar bear camera that streams from Churchill, Manitoba, one of the best places to see polar bears in the wild. You can watch these powerful animals as they roam the snowy tundra, hunt for food, and interact with each other. It's like having a front-row seat to the daily life of polar bears.

The World Wildlife Fund (WWF) also offers live Arctic webcams, showing animals like walruses, caribou, and even Arctic foxes. These webcams are usually set up during specific seasons when animals are most active, giving viewers a chance to see them during important times, like migration or breeding. Watching animals on live cameras is a great way to feel connected to the Arctic's wildlife, even if you're thousands of miles away. It also gives you a better understanding of how these animals survive in such a harsh environment and why it's important to protect their habitat.

For a more interactive experience, try out some online games and activities that focus on the Arctic. National Geographic Kids offers several games and quizzes that teach you about Arctic animals, geography, and climate. You can play a game where you match animals to their habitats, take a quiz to find out how much you know about the Arctic, or even learn about the challenges of climate change through fun, interactive activities. These games make learning about the Arctic feel like an adventure, combining fun with education.

Many museums also offer online resources and activities about the Arctic. The Smithsonian Museum of Natural History has a special Arctic exhibit with virtual tours, videos, and activities. You can explore the history of Arctic exploration, learn about the people who have lived there for thousands of years, and see artifacts that show how they survived in such a cold environment. They even have 3D models of Arctic animals and tools used by Indigenous Arctic communities, so you can see these items up close from your computer. It's like having a museum visit without having to leave home.

If you enjoy videos and documentaries, YouTube and other streaming platforms have a wealth of Arctic-related content. BBC Earth, National Geographic, and many other organizations have created incredible documentaries about the Arctic, covering everything from polar bears and seals to the effects of climate change. Watching these videos gives you a chance to see the Arctic's breathtaking landscapes and learn from scientists who study the region. Some videos even show scientists doing research in the Arctic, like drilling into glaciers, studying polar bears, or measuring the thickness of sea ice. Seeing their work up close helps you understand why the Arctic is such an important place for science and conservation.

For those interested in real-time science, NASA and the National Oceanic and Atmospheric Administration (NOAA) both have websites dedicated to Arctic research. These sites offer live data about the Arctic's ice cover, weather, and climate conditions, which scientists use to monitor changes in the Arctic. You can see maps that show how much sea ice is present at different times of the year, learn about the Arctic's temperature changes, and explore interactive tools that let you track changes over time. This kind of data helps scientists understand how the Arctic is responding to climate change, and by exploring these resources, you can see the same information that researchers use in their studies.

Social media is another great way to explore the Arctic, as many Arctic researchers, conservation organizations, and photographers share their experiences online. You can follow scientists who work in the Arctic to see their photos, videos, and stories from the field. Some scientists even answer questions from kids, giving you a chance to learn directly from the people who study this region. Conservation groups like WWF and the Arctic Institute post regular updates about Arctic wildlife, environmental challenges, and the latest scientific discoveries. It's an easy way to stay connected and learn something new every day.

One of the most powerful ways to explore the Arctic from home is by reading books and articles about it. There are many books written for kids that explain the Arctic's unique environment, animals, and people. Some books focus on specific animals, like polar bears or Arctic foxes, while others cover the history of Arctic exploration or the effects of climate change on the region. Reading allows you to explore the Arctic in depth, and it sparks your imagination, helping you picture the frozen landscapes, northern lights, and wildlife that make the Arctic so special.

For a creative way to learn about the Arctic, try writing your own Arctic adventure story or drawing pictures of Arctic animals and landscapes. Imagine you're an explorer setting out on an Arctic expedition, encountering polar bears, icebergs, and the northern lights along the way. You could draw scenes of glaciers, icy mountains, or animals in the tundra, capturing the beauty and mystery of this region. Creating your own Arctic art or stories can be a fun way to bring what you've learned to life and share it with friends and family.

Finally, learning about the Arctic from home reminds us of how connected we all are to this incredible place. Even though the Arctic might seem distant, its health affects the entire planet, from the air we breathe to the oceans that surround us. By exploring the Arctic through virtual field trips, videos, and online resources, we not only satisfy our curiosity but also gain a deeper understanding of why it's so important to protect this unique region.

Activities to Try

The Arctic is full of wonders, from the way snow and ice cover the land to the incredible wildlife that calls it home. Even if you can't visit the Arctic in person, you can bring some of its magic right into your home with fun, hands-on activities. By experimenting with snow and ice, or creating Arctic-themed crafts, you'll get a taste of what it's like in the far north and learn more about this fascinating region. Let's dive into a few DIY snow experiments and Arctic crafts that will make you feel like an Arctic explorer right from your own space.

One of the most exciting ways to explore Arctic science is by experimenting with ice and snow. If it's winter and there's snow outside, you're in luck! You can collect some real snow to use in your experiments. But if you don't have snow, don't worry – you can make your own snow at home with a few simple ingredients. To start, here's a recipe for DIY snow that feels soft and fluffy, just like the real thing. All you need is baking soda and shaving cream. In a bowl, mix about two cups of baking soda with shaving cream, adding the shaving cream a little at a time until you get a snowy texture. The mixture should be cold to the touch, just like real snow, and you can mold it into small snowballs or a mini snowman.

Another fun snow experiment is learning about how Arctic animals stay warm. Polar bears, seals, and whales have a layer of fat called blubber that keeps them insulated in the cold. To simulate blubber, try the "blubber glove" experiment. You'll need a bowl of ice water, two plastic bags, and a handful of vegetable shortening. First, spread the shortening inside one of the plastic bags, coating it as evenly as possible. Then, put your hand in the other plastic bag and slide it into the bag with shortening, making sure there's a thick layer of "blubber" between your hand and the cold water. Dip your hand in the ice water and see how the "blubber" keeps your hand warm. Compare it to putting your hand in the water without the blubber glove. This experiment is a fun way to feel just how effective blubber is at keeping Arctic animals warm.

If you're curious about how icebergs float, try making your own mini icebergs. Fill a bowl with water and freeze a few small containers of water to create ice blocks. Once the ice has frozen, remove it from the containers and place the ice blocks in the water. Watch how they float, with most of the ice underwater and only a small part sticking out. This is similar to how real icebergs float in the Arctic Ocean. You can even add a few drops of blue food coloring to the water to make it look like the Arctic Ocean. Notice how much of the "iceberg" stays below the surface. Most people are surprised to learn that about 90% of an iceberg is underwater, which makes icebergs look much smaller than they actually are!

After experimenting with ice, try making an

Arctic diorama to create your own little world of snow and ice. For this craft, you'll need a small box (like a shoebox), white paint, cotton balls, and some Arctic animal figurines or printed pictures of polar bears, seals, and Arctic foxes. Start by painting the inside of the box white, to mimic the snowy Arctic landscape. Then, glue cotton balls around the bottom of the box to create fluffy snow. If you want to add an "ice" effect, you can cut pieces of blue plastic or use small chunks of clear plastic to represent frozen lakes or icy patches. Place your animal figurines or pictures inside the box, arranging them to look like a little Arctic scene. You can even add a small light to represent the northern lights shining over your Arctic world.

If you love art, try making your own northern lights painting. The northern lights are one of the most magical sights in the Arctic, with colors that dance across the night sky. To create your own version of the aurora, you'll need black or dark blue paper and oil pastels or chalk. Start by drawing swirls, waves, and lines with bright colors like green, pink, purple, and yellow. Blend the colors gently with your fingers to create a soft, glowing effect. The darker the background, the brighter your colors will look, making it seem like the lights are shining in the night sky. For extra sparkle, sprinkle a little glitter on top to mimic the stars that often shine alongside the aurora. Display your artwork and imagine watching the northern lights on a cold Arctic night.

To learn about Arctic animals and their footprints, try making animal track stamps. In the snow, animals leave behind unique footprints that tell a story of where they've been and what they're doing. To make your own stamps, you'll need small pieces of foam or sponge, glue, and small blocks of wood or cardboard to attach your stamps. Look up pictures of Arctic animal tracks, like the paw prints of a polar bear, the hooves of a caribou, or the flipper tracks of a seal. Cut out shapes from the foam that match these tracks and glue each one onto a block. Once your stamps are dry, press them into a pad of washable paint and stamp them onto a sheet of paper to create an Arctic animal trail. See if you can follow the tracks and imagine where each animal was going!

Snowflakes are another fascinating part of the Arctic. Each snowflake is unique, and you can create your own paper snowflakes to decorate your home. Start by folding a piece of paper into a triangle several times, then cut out shapes along the edges. When you unfold the paper, you'll have a beautiful, one-of-a-kind snowflake. You can make snowflakes of different sizes and hang them in your room or on the windows to create a wintery Arctic scene. For an added Arctic effect, you can sprinkle some glitter on your snowflakes to make them sparkle like real snow.

If you enjoy learning about the Arctic's animals, make your own Arctic animal mask. Choose your favorite Arctic animal – whether it's a polar bear, Arctic fox, or snowy owl – and gather paper, markers, and string. Draw the shape of the animal's face on a piece of paper, cut it out, and add details like eyes, a nose, and fur patterns. Attach a piece of string to either side of the mask so you can wear it and "become" your favorite Arctic animal. Try acting out how the animal might behave in the Arctic, like the quiet stalking of an Arctic fox or the graceful glide of a snowy owl through the snow-covered landscape.

Lastly, try making a simple Arctic survival kit. Imagine you're going on an expedition to the Arctic, and think about what you might need to stay warm and safe. Using a small box, gather items like a pair of gloves, a small flashlight, a map, and maybe even a notebook for recording your Arctic "discoveries." This can be a pretend kit, where you fill the box with drawings or pictures of these items, or you can collect real items from around your home. Thinking about the gear needed to explore the Arctic helps you understand just how tough and prepared you'd need to be for a real Arctic adventure.

Milton Keynes UK
Ingram Content Group UK Ltd.
UKHW021929201124
451474UK00014B/1005

9 798330 558179